SECRET LONDON

UNUSUAL BARS & RESTAURANTS

Rachel Howard

Photographs: Jorge Monedero

Cover illustration: Alice Charbin

Jonglez Publishing

London is full of fashionable restaurants and bars, their turnover fuelled by a relentless PR machine that tells locals where to go to see and be seen. This guide is an antidote to food fads, molecular mixologists and celebrity chefs who have morphed into multinational brands. It's a collection of unusual places in unlikely locations, independent businesses kept afloat by eccentric owners, local institutions oblivious to passing trends.

From hidden canteens to underground drinking dens, the food and drink isn't always the most memorable thing about these places. Their diversity – a Thai greasy spoon, a 1950s' ballroom, a cabaret club in a public convenience – reflects the cosmopolitan spirit of London, a city that champions the unconventional despite being steeped in tradition.

It took a long time to whittle down the final selection, aided by many intrepid dining and drinking partners, whose curiosity, enthusiasm and tolerance for bad meals knew no bounds. For every place that made the grade, several others were reviewed and ultimately rejected – too trendy, tacky, classic, unwelcoming, or downright ghastly. I'm sure there are many more unsung secrets that I've yet to discover, but eventually I had to end my quest because I became pregnant. At least I know my son won't be a fussy eater.

Rachel Howard

p. 106

✈ London Luton Airport

Kenton

Hendon

Archway

North Circular

Finchley

Hendon

Road

Brent Reservoir

Wembley Stadium

Way

Parliament Hill

Road

Gladstone Park

Hampstead

Wembley

Circular

North

Willesden

Haverstock Hill

Road

Primrose Hill

Can

p. 70

Regent's Park

King's C St Panc

Park

Euston

Wormwood Scrubs Park

Westway

Marylebone

Marylebone Rd

Blooms

Westway

Notting Hill

Bayswater

Paddington

Mayfair

Soh

Acton

Hyde Park

Charing C

St Jan

Warwick

Buckingham Palace

Westmi

✈ London Heathrow Airport

Kensington

Belgravia

Victoria Station

Gunnersbury Park

Chiswick High

Rd

Great

Rd

Finborough

Chelsea

Kings

Pimlico

Cedars Rd

Ellesmere Rd

West Rd

Fulham Palace

Rd

Battersea Park

KEW BRIDGE

Castelnau

HAMMERSMITH BRIDGE

Thames

Fulham

King's

BATTERSEA BRIDGE

New Co Garden Ma

CHISWICK BRIDGE

Church Rd

PUTNEY BRIDGE

WANDSWORTH

Clapha

Lower Mortlake Rd

Lower Richmond Rd

Upper

Richmond

Rd

King's

Clapham Junction

Clapham Common

Putney

Hill

Trinity

Balham

Richmond Park

West

Merton Rd

Garratt

Balham High

Rd

Kingston Rd

Wimbledon Park Side

Durnford Rd

Lane

Mitcham

Tooting High St

Tooting Bec

Roehampton Vale

Wimbledon Park

Robin

Parkside High St.

Kingston Hill

Kingston Vale

Hood

Wimbledon Common

Wimbledon

Rd

Haydons Rd

Merantun W.

Western

Rd

London

Streatham

Mitcham

Rd

Coombe Ln

Worple

Rd

Kingston

Rd

Merton

Mitcha

Kingston

Bushey

Rd

p. 152

↙ ✈ London Gatwick Airport

London Stansted Airport ✈

Tottenham

Walthamstow

Wanstead

Hornsey

Green Road

Seven Sisters

Finsbury Park

West Reservoir

Stamford Hill

Clapton Common

Upr Clapton Rd

Lea Bridge

Road

Leyton

Wanstead Park

N

Stoke Newington

Cross Route

East Cross

Canonbury

St Paul's Rd

Balls Pond Rd

Graham Rd

Homerton High St.

Hackney

East Cross Rd

Stratford

East Ham

Islington

Kingsland Rd

Hackney Rd

Victoria Park

West Ham

Road

Hoxton

City Rd

Bethnal Gr. Rd

Bow Rd

Barking

Finsbury

Clerkenwell

Liverpool St.

Mile End

Rd

Barnet Rd

Blackwall Tunnel Northern Appr.

Newham

Way

Holborn

Blackfriars

Whitechapel

City

Commercial Rd

East India Dock Road

Millenium Dome

Royal Victoria Dock

Cannon St.

Tower of London

Canary Wharf

London City Airport ✈

Waterloo

LONDON BRIDGE

TOWER BRIDGE

London Bridge

Thames

Isle of Dogs

Manchester Rd

ELEPHANT AND CASTLE

Bermondsey

Evelyn St.

Kennington Park Rd

Old Kent Rd

Burgess Park

Deptford

Greenwich

Camberwell New Rd

Camberwell

Peckham Rd

New Cross Rd

Greenwich High Rd

Greenwich Park

Rd

Rochester Way

Brixton

Denmark Rd

East Dulwich Rd

Evelina Rd

Peckham Rye Park

Shooters Hill

Ruskin Park

Lee

High

Eltham

Rochester Way Ave.

Brockwell Park

Crosted Rd

Dulwich Park

Brockley Rd

Lewisham

Westhorne

Sidcup

Eltham Hill

Court Rd

Norwood Rd

S. Croxted Rd

Dulwich Common

London Rd

Stanstead Rd

Brownhill Rd

Baring

Rd

Streatham

Westwood Hill

Crystal Palace Park

Sydenham Rd

Southend Ln

Bromley Rd

Beckenham Place Park

Sundridge Park

Norwood

Beulah Hill

Central Hill

Church Rd

Crystal Palace

Anerley Rd

Beckenham

0   2   4 km

0   1   2 miles

CONTENTS

CONTENTS

CENTRAL LONDON

PAOLINA'S THAI CAFÉ

181 King's Cross Road, King's Cross, WC1X 9BZ
- 020 7278 8176
- Open Mon–Fri 12–3pm and 6–10pm, Sat 6–10pm; closed Sun
- Transport King's Cross tube
- Budget

> *Cheap dates and hot noodles*

I lived around the corner from this place for a couple of years, and I must have eaten here at least 50 times. Yet my next-door neighbour, who had lived in the area for a decade, had never heard of it. Perhaps that's because Paolina sure isn't a looker at first glance. Hurrying along this dingy stretch of King's Cross Road, it would be easy to overlook the faded yellow shop front with its wobbly hand-drawn sign. Even if you peered through the doorway, you probably wouldn't be tempted inside: the cluttered kitchen at the front looks like an unsavoury takeaway. But venture in and you'll be pleasantly surprised.

Squeeze past the smiling chefs, sweating over steaming vats of noodles, and you'll discover a tiny dining room hidden at the rear. (Tinier still is the WC – surely the smallest in London?) Wood-panelled, with no windows, the restaurant is cosiest on frosty evenings. The same plastic flowers, Formica tables and portraits of Thai royalty appear to have been there since the 1970s, although in fact this Thai café opened in 1996. Prior to that, it was an Italian caff run by the eponymous Paolina. The new owners didn't bother to change the name as they couldn't afford a new sign. But it's Celia (who claims her real Thai name is unpronounceable) who has run the show ever since.

Punters are packed in tight but there's always a buzzy, easy camaraderie. Most diners are regulars who come for the pitch-perfect pad Thai and fantastically friendly service. Paolina's is family-run and the food tastes like home cooking. Starters rely heavily on the deep fryer, so I usually stick to hot and sour soups such as *tom kha gai* (chicken, coconut milk, lemongrass and lime leaves) or red-hot salads such as *som tum* (papaya with chillies, ground peanuts and dried shrimp). Curries won't blow your brains out as they do in many Thai restaurants, which is good news for chilli lightweights like me. But it's the stir-fried dishes that stand out – particularly that pad Thai.

This is one of those rare London restaurants where you can have a fine supper for a tenner. You can bring your own booze; the corkage charge is just 50p. Call me a cheap date, but in my book Paolina's is perfect for a romantic rendezvous. The cheerful welcome was one of the things I missed most when I moved out of King's Cross. I was saddened to discover on my last visit that the beaming, bespectacled owner had died. But Celia is still manning the woks and everything else remains reassuringly unchanged.

CORAM CAFÉ

The Foundling Museum, 40 Brunswick Square, Bloomsbury, WC1N 1AZ
• 020 7841 3609
• www.foundlingmuseum.org.uk/visit-us/cafe/
• Open Tues–Sat 10am–4.45pm, Sun 11am–4.45pm (lunch orders until 3pm); closed Mon
• Transport Russell Square tube
• Budget

> *Kids, cakes and classical music*

There's a rather good Austrian café in Coram Fields, a 7 acre park with a miniature farm bang in the middle of Bloomsbury. But there's a hitch: adults can only access the divine Viennese pastries at Kipferl café (open March–Nov, 10am–5pm, www.kipferl.co.uk) if accompanied by a child. Coram Fields is the only park in London where adults unattended by a child under 16 are forbidden to enter. (As a consolation for the childless, Kipferl also operates a hot-dog stand in Bloomsbury's Gordon Square, serving authentic German sausages smothered in mustard.)

London's first public playground, Coram Fields was established in 1936 on the former site of the Foundling Hospital, a refuge for abandoned, orphaned or destitute children founded by Thomas Coram in 1739. There's a poignant contrast between the laughter of children today and the mournful tales of the 25,000 infants once taken into care here, whose memories and memorabilia are displayed at the Foundling Museum, discreetly positioned behind the park. The museum also contains an exceptional collection of paintings by William Hogarth, a founding Governor of the Hospital, who also encouraged many of his contemporaries to donate works. His efforts were so successful that the children's sanctuary soon became London's first public art gallery.

Another major benefactor was George Frideric Handel, who gave a benefit performance of *Messiah* every year from 1749 until his death a decade later. True to this tradition, classical recitals are often staged in the splendid Picture Gallery, with free admission for museum ticket holders.

Even if you're too mean to fork out for a ticket, you can listen to Classic FM in the Coram Café, a bright, white space with picture windows framing leafy Brunswick Square. Despite the red leather and chrome chairs, it feels rather like a school refectory. Even the short menu of comfort food is seemingly designed to appeal to hungry teenagers (or burnt-out parents in need of a sugar hit). There are more cakes than at a kids' party, as well as wholesome soups, pies and sandwiches. After a long wait, my cheddar, tomato and chutney toastie arrived badly charred – with no apology – but it was still surprisingly tasty. Scones with clotted cream and strawberry jam were perfectly poised between crumbly and claggy.

As you leave, look out for Tracey Emin's bronze cast of a baby mitten on the railings outside the museum, another touching reminder of the young lives changed by this institution.

INDIAN YMCA

41 Fitzroy Square, Fitzrovia, W1T 6AQ
• 020 7387 0411
• www.indianymca.org
• Open Mon–Fri noon–2pm, 7–8.30pm, weekends and bank holidays
12.30–1.30pm, 7–8.30pm
• Transport Warren Street, Euston Square or Goodge Street tube
• Budget

Curry favour

Youth hostels aren't places I'd normally associate with good food. If YMCA brings to mind Village People rather than hot dinners, you'll be surprised by this odd little anachronism in north west, north, north east & east. Founded in 1920 to provide cheap accommodation for Indian students in London, the Indian YMCA has survived several incarnations. These premises on Fitzroy Square were officially opened by the High Commissioner of India in 1953. Even Nehru came to give his blessing. In 1962, this became London's first mixed-sex youth hostel, a surprisingly racy move for such a conservative establishment.

In all other respects, the atmosphere at this charming time warp is comfortingly institutional. In the cafeteria, impoverished students hunch over heaped plates of dirt-cheap curry alongside thrifty academics, office workers and Indian expats pining for a taste of home. Attentive staff in white jackets and hats chitchat with the regulars in Hindi. The room bears all the hallmarks of a canteen in any sub-continental backwater, right down to the Formica tables, beige curtains, neon lighting, and a washbasin for traditionalists who prefer to eschew cutlery.

Fine dining, this ain't. It's self-service. Vats of mutton, prawn, and chicken curry look fairly indistinguishable, but they're all tasty and freshly made. A mound of pilau rice, ferociously spiced cabbage and lentil curry, onion bhajis, and saucers of chutney and raita will set you back a fiver. Drinks are limited to mango lassi and jugs of tap water on every table. Ghee is used sparingly, so the food doesn't leave a greasy aftertaste despite the giant servings.

The cafeteria is open for just a few hours each day. There's a lunch-break rush around 1pm, so go earlier or later to be sure of a seat. It's not a place for a leisurely meal, but it's ideal for eating alone.

The rooms upstairs are a bargain too, although I'm not sure the lodgings will inspire the same enthusiasm as the restaurant. A pile of mattresses was wedged between the toilets and the coffee-dispensing machine on my last visit.

NEARBY

ARCHIPELAGO
(110 Whitfield Street, Fitzrovia, W1T 5ED; 020 7383 3346;
www.archipelago-restaurant.co.uk)
Everything about this restaurant is self-consciously quirky: the wine list comes in a cage, the bill arrives in a treasure chest, and there are garlic locusts, chocolate-covered scorpions, kangaroo and crocodile on the menu. Beware of ordering "a visit from the doctor"…

ODIN'S

4

27 Devonshire Street, Marylebone, W1G 6PL
• 020 7935 7296 • www.langansrestaurants.co.uk
• Open Mon–Fri noon–2.30pm, 6.30–11pm, Sat 6.30–11pm,
Sun noon–4pm
• Transport Great Portland Street tube
• Expensive (but good value set menus)

*Don't order
sambuca*

You could walk past Odin's dozens of times without realising that a slice of London history lies behind the net curtains. Only the hand-drawn menu hints at the astonishing art collection inside. Drawings and paintings by the likes of David Hockney, Patrick Procktor, R.B. Kitaj and Laura Knight cover every inch of wall space. Several portray the crumpled features of Peter Langan, the ebullient Irishman who bought the restaurant in 1966. Up-and-coming artists donated pictures in exchange for boozy lunches at Odin's and the smaller, less formal Langan's Bistro next door.

Deeply unfashionable yet desperately romantic, Odin's is a time warp. Wall-mounted lamps cast a soft-focus glow over starched linens. There's no muzak, only the clink of solid silver on vintage china and the purring of well-fed patrons. Capacious seats are comforting, just like the cheese on toast proffered by heavy-set waiters with thick Slavic accents. Co-owner Michael Caine once held court here. After their partnership broke down, Langan described Caine as a "mediocrity with halitosis". Caine retorted: "You would have a more interesting conversation with a cabbage." Today, the sole proprietor is Michelin-starred chef Richard Shepherd, who joined Langan's in 1977. The Anglo-French menu is a homage to that era. "No, the chef didn't fall asleep thirty years ago," our waiter, Rocky (real name Radovan) assured us. "People like the food, so why change it?" Daily specials – honey roast gammon on Wednesdays, roast beef on Thursdays – reinforce the sense of dining in an institution. It's the kind of place where waiters ask: "English or French mustard, sir?"

The food is surprisingly good. Smoked haddock soufflé tasted like posh baby food, enlivened by fiery horseradish sauce. Sea bass with roast fennel was winningly paired with rich sweet potato mash. I couldn't resist ordering Irish coffee alongside rhubarb crumble with *crème anglaise* (a euphemism for custard). Until they brought out the *petits fours*, I hadn't seen a doily for decades.

Although some things haven't changed, the atmosphere is more sedate than it was in Langan's heyday. Langan, who allegedly drank a dozen bottles of champagne a day, would vomit on customers, cut off their ties, and pass out on tabletops. He grilled female diners about their sexual preferences or crawled under the table and nibbled their ankles. Our waiter told us that Langan died accidentally trying to light a cigar while drinking flaming sambuca. In fact, Langan was trying to set fire to his estranged wife, whom he lured into a wardrobe full of petrol with the promise of sex. Shepherd has banned restaurant critics after unfavourable reviews. I do hope he doesn't take offence, as I really don't want to be blacklisted from this classy joint.

RIBA RESTAURANT AND CAFÉ ⑤

66 Portland Place, Fitzrovia, W1B 1AD
• 020 7631 0467
• www.architecture.com
• Open Restaurant Mon–Fri noon–3pm, Tues 5.30–9.30pm; Café Mon–Fri 8am–6pm
• Transport Great Portland Street or Oxford Circus tube
• Moderate

> ### *Inspired food in an inspiring setting*

I've often wandered past the magnificent embassies on Portland Place and wondered what lavish banquets are underway within their soaring halls. Edward Davenport turned this fantasy into a lucrative business, renting out 33 Portland Place for film shoots and orgies – until his conviction for fraud abruptly ended the party.

Those of us who aren't ambassadors, celebrities or sex kittens can get a taste of the Portland Place high life at RIBA, the Royal Institute of British Architects. Founded in 1834, RIBA's current headquarters opened a century later. The six-storey building faced in Portland stone is minimalist and effortlessly modern: there's no gilt, no patterned carpets, no imposing portraits on the walls. Massive bronze doors, decorated with a relief of London's riverside landmarks, lead to a grand marble and glass staircase. On the first floor, four colossal black

marble columns demarcate the atrium café. Etched glass doors open onto the elegant dining room.

There's a perfect geometry and harmony to the space. Carved reliefs depicting "man and his buildings through the ages" decorate the ceiling and window piers. Semi-circular banquettes and leather and chrome chairs are positioned near the floor-to-ceiling windows, leaving the central space free for temporary exhibitions. During the summer, the windows open onto a beautifully landscaped terrace with living walls – perfect for a clandestine date, especially on Tuesday evenings when the restaurant is open for dinner.

Unlike so many museum cafés, this isn't just an excuse to make a quick buck by serving soggy sandwiches at inflated prices. It's a proper restaurant, with superb service and relatively modest prices (especially the set menus). The seasonal, sustainably minded British menu is refreshed monthly, which pleases the regulars – mostly architects, Harley Street doctors and BBC executives.

Creamy chestnut soup was accompanied by an irresistible selection of breads. Bright orange pumpkin risotto came with a crispy centrepiece of fried Wigmore cheese, ringed by sage and sorrel. A deconstructed game pie topped with a suspended pastry roof was served on a slate, with a smear of piccalilli and a slab of pâté. Portions are generous and presentation is architectural. Elaborate desserts are equally ambitious, but you can't go wrong with the selection of British cheeses and chutneys.

Afterwards, browse the architecture library on the third floor, which holds over 150,000 books, 1.5 million photographs, and even a fragment of Sir Christopher Wren's coffin.

OCTOBER GALLERY

24 Old Gloucester Street, Bloomsbury, WC1N 3AL
- 020 7242 7367
- www.octobergallery.co.uk
- Open Café: Tues–Fri 12.30–1.30pm; Gallery: Tues–Sat 12.30–5.30pm; closed August
- Transport Holborn or Russell Square tube
- Budget

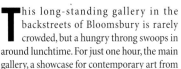

Iranian artistry

This long-standing gallery in the backstreets of Bloomsbury is rarely crowded, but a hungry throng swoops in around lunchtime. For just one hour, the main gallery, a showcase for contemporary art from all over the world, morphs into a dining room where the Middle Eastern menu changes daily. The Iranian chef Khosrow Jalavind ("Kes") serves a beautiful spread of five or six Persian dishes – perhaps jewelled rice with pomegranates and pistachios, chicken stewed in walnut and pomegranate sauce, vegetables lightly steamed with saffron, spiced grilled aubergines, and creamy lentil and dill puree, garnished with yoghurt, tarragon and shallot sauce. It's a feast of rich but subtle flavours, all for a very reasonable set price including fruit juice and a side salad. No wonder Kes' regulars prefer to keep this place a secret.

"In the Iranian army, my first job was to distribute food to 400 soldiers in less than an hour," Kes recalls. Feeding 25 or 30 people must seem like a breeze in comparison. "Yes, but I'm heartbroken if I run out of food and have to turn people away," he says. (Show up early to be sure.) Kes learned to cook when he was posted to a remote village in the desert, experimenting with whatever meagre ingredients were available. "I was the only soldier who could cook, so every Friday I used to make a big meal for all the troops."

An industrial chemist, he came to Britain to escape the repressive regime. "My background in chemistry has been useful: I pick and mix different ingredients so all the flavours and textures work in harmony."

On sunny afternoons, food is served in the glorious walled courtyard, a leafy oasis paved with red and black tiles. The building, which dates from 1863, was originally a Church of England school. The garden overlooked the Ospedale Italiano, founded for the Italian immigrants of Soho. Schoolgirls had to lower their eyes so they wouldn't glimpse the patients in their pyjamas. When the October Gallery moved here in 1979, the building was derelict. Founding director Chilli Hawes discovered an apothecary in the cellar and underground tunnels, allegedly used to deliver food to King George III while he was being treated for madness at a clinic on Queens Square. To compensate for all the "blood-letting, purging and blistering" the king had to endure, his wife, Queen Charlotte, stored his favourite delicacies in the cellar of a nearby pub, named The Queen's Larder in her honour.

CAMERA CAFÉ

44 Museum Street, Bloomsbury, WC1A 1LY
• 07887 930826
• www.cameracafe.co.uk
• Open Mon–Fri 11am–7pm, Sat noon–7pm
• Transport Tottenham Court Road or Holborn tube
• Moderate

Use your noodle

The backstreets opposite the British Museum aren't just crawling with tourists. Professional photographers scour the area's camera shops for specialist gear. Behind the cabinets of second-hand Leicas, Nikons and Hasselblads on sale at Aperture is this tiny café, run by amateur snapper and chilli lover Adrian Tang.

His quirky coffee shop has been around since 1999 in various guises. First it was Tang, then The Museum Café, "but tourists kept coming in asking where the entrance to the British Museum was." Tang tried his hand at poetry nights until eventually he hit upon the idea of adding a camera shop to boost business. Some of the regulars are camera buffs. Others come for Tang's excellent classical and jazz collection, tip-tapping away on their laptops taking advantage of the free wifi. (There are a couple of computers for hire too). Space is tight, with just a handful of tables in the bright red back room or basement, but you could stay for hours and nobody would mind.

As well as a predictable selection of sandwiches, Adrian serves tasty (though rather pricy and oddly garnished with limp lettuce leaves) vegetable, chicken, or prawn *chow mein*, served with his own homemade Happy Buddha chilli oil. There are freshly pressed juices, fancy coffees and herbal infusions, including brown rice tea – definitely an acquired taste.

There are a few old magazines and board games, but surprisingly no photography books. The only photos on the walls are generic prints of Marilyn Monroe and Mick Jagger. The rest of the wall space is covered in random posters, hand-drawn cartoons, and bamboo steamers. The furniture has seen better days, the whole place is pretty scruffy, but there's a strange charm and sense of calm that seduces you. The electric guitar by the bar was a gift from a customer. "I only play it when it's really empty," says Tang. "Otherwise everyone would leave."

NEARBY

LONDON REVIEW CAKE SHOP
(14 Bury Place, Bloomsbury, WC1A 2JL; 020 7269 9030; www.lrbshop.co.uk/cakeshop)
Wander through the history section of this inspiring bookshop and you'll find an elegant café that serves fabulous Monmouth coffee, Jing and Mariage Frères teas, and all sorts of irresistible treats (the blueberry cake is heavenly). Savoury dishes – sweet potato and feta stew, celeriac soup with thyme pesto – are just as good. Most customers are quietly engrossed in the books and periodicals scattered about the communal tables.

COURT RESTAURANT

British Museum, Great Russell Street, Bloomsbury, WC1B 3DG
- 020 7323 8990
- www.britishmuseum.org/visiting/eat/court_restaurant.aspx
- Open Daily for lunch noon–3pm, afternoon tea 3–5.30pm, dinner 5.30–8pm Fri only
- Transport Holborn, Russell Square or Goodge Street tube
- Moderate

> *Art-inspired menus*

Norman Foster's Great Court has transformed the British Museum from a fusty old fogey into a modern icon. In Robert Smirke's original design, the museum courtyard was imagined as an exotic botanical garden. But when the round Reading Room (inspired by Rome's Pantheon and frequented by Karl Marx and Bram Stoker) was installed in 1857, the courtyard was closed to the public. Foster's ingenious £100 million makeover encased this dead space in a glass and steel dome, a puzzle of 3,312 triangular panes of which no two are the same. The diffused light casts an ethereal glow over the two-acre Great Court – the largest enclosed public space in Europe.

Wrapped around the Reading Room, a pair of white stone staircases seems to lead up into the sky. In fact, they lead to the Court Restaurant, a circular space concealed beneath the dome. High above the swarming cafés and shops at ground level, the discreet dining room – all charcoal grey, chocolate brown, and starched white linen – creates a neutral backdrop for the neoclassical columns and porticos that surround it.

"It's a very academic crowd," said my companion approvingly. Not too flash, just buzzy enough, the room hums with erudite chatter. It's just the place to impress potential clients or visiting in-laws.

My companion chose to brave the Exhibition Menu, themed around the current show by the cross-dressing potter Grayson Perry. The artist's motorbike tour of Germany, accompanied by his teddy bear, is the unlikely inspiration for an edifying *Rinderbrühe* (beef consommé with miniature slices of steak daubed with floating mushrooms) and chicken schnitzel served with dainty sides of Teutonic potatoes, cucumber and pickled cabbage. I plumped for more traditional British fare: a rich parsnip soup with glazed apples and celeriac crisp that hovered between sweet and earthy, and lemon sole with olive and thyme mashed potato, steamed spinach and lime butter. Both the presentation and service of every dish was quietly graceful. Only the desserts seem overly fussy – tangerine panna cotta with hot berry ragout, mini apple-walnut crostata and vanilla sorbet was a riot of clashing flavours that even Grayson Perry would baulk at. A trio of pear, blackberry and lemon sorbets was refreshingly simple.

The restaurant also serves afternoon tea and early dinner on Friday evenings. I can't think of a better way to kick off the weekend than a stroll through the Middle Eastern galleries followed by a pink gin fizz.

ARCHITECTURAL ASSOCIATION DINING ROOM ❾

36 Bedford Square, Bloomsbury, WC1B 3ES
• 020 7887 4091 • www.aaschool.ac.uk
• Open Dining room: Mon—Fri 12.15—4.30pm, Sat 10am—4.30pm;
bar: Mon—Fri 9.15am—5pm
• Transport Tottenham Court Road or Goodge Street tube
• Budget

*Chic
and cheap*

O f all Bloomsbury's beautiful garden squares, Bedford Square is perhaps the loveliest. The Architectural Association's School of Architecture, which occupies a whole sweep of Georgian splendour on the western side of the square, is surely one of the most elegant campuses anywhere in London. Founded in 1847, the AA opened as a day school in 1901 and moved to Bedford Square in 1917.

Faculties are split between ten townhouses, but No. 36 is the school's public face. Students' work in progress is displayed around the building. The elegant ground-floor parlour has been converted into an exhibition space, which hosts architecture, interior design and photography. The work is eclectic but always fascinating: Gio Ponti chairs, temporary structures fashioned by homeless Americans, the unbuilt architecture of London.

Exhibitions often spill over into the first floor bar. With cheap beers and bay windows overlooking Bedford Square, it's the kind of place where you could easily lose a whole afternoon. Hidden at the back is a terrace where you can bunk off work and nobody will find you.

Although it's open to the public, you'd never know there was a dining room in the basement. There's nothing to alert visitors to its existence. The big, bright room is characteristically well designed (by one of the AA's tutors), with a black floor, plain wooden chairs and large tables in block colours. Lunch, prepared by long-standing chef Pascal Babeau, is laid out on a mosaic counter. The self-service salad selection raises the bar: there's no limp lettuce or soggy sweetcorn here; it's all Asian noodles, spinach, beetroot and grapefruit, and just grated coleslaw. There are two or three hot meals, which might be tomato, olive and mozzarella quiche, mushroom casserole or beef curry served with rice. It's unbeatable value: hefty portions of home cooking at supermarket prices in stylish surroundings. Go early to avoid disappointment: after 2.15pm (and on Saturdays), they only serve gourmet sandwiches (try the Parma ham, parmesan, sun blush tomatoes and salad) and pizzas.

NEARBY

BRADLEY'S SPANISH BAR
(42—44 Hanway Street, Fitzrovia, W1T 1UP; 020 7636 0359; www.bradleysspanishbar.co.uk)
Among the many late-night Spanish dives on Hanway Street, Bradley's is easily the most appealing. This cramped, chaotic, delightful bar has one of the last surviving vinyl jukeboxes in London. The rotating collection of singles spans everything from The Supremes to The White Stripes.

WEEKEND SUPPER AT THE WALLACE COLLECTION

⑩

Hertford House, Manchester Square, Marylebone, W1U 3BN
• 0207 563 9505
• www.thewallacerestaurant.co.uk
• Open Sun–Thurs 10am–5pm (last orders 4.30pm), Fri, Sat 10am–11pm (last orders 9.30pm)
• Transport Bond Street or Baker Street tube
• Expensive

> *The kind of place where you can't resist ordering a glass of champagne*

The Victoria & Albert was the world's first museum with a public restaurant, offering first-, second- and third-class menus depending on the visitor's social status. The Wallace Collection's restaurant seems to be designed squarely with the upper crust in mind. In a soaring, salmon-pink courtyard, this elegant brasserie is hidden inside a stately home stuffed with old masters, suits of armour, and all manner of trifles and trinkets.

Hertford House, a huge pile just behind Oxford Street, belonged to the Marquesses of Hertford, a succession of reprobates with refined tastes who amassed a vast collection of 18th- and 19th-century art and antiques. The 25 rooms are decked out as they would have been while the aristocrats were in residence: with clashing wallpaper, lashings of porcelain, and old masters by Rembrandt, Rubens, Velázquez and Van Dyck. When British Prime Minister Benjamin Disraeli signed the visitors' book in 1878, he described it as a "palace of genius, fancy and taste". Bequeathed to the nation in 1897, the collection also includes one of the largest arrays of armour in the UK (visitors can try on chain mail for size in the Conservation Gallery). One room is filled with furniture that belonged to Queen Marie-Antoinette of France.

The Wallace Restaurant is rather like being transported to the court of Versailles – or, at least, a Parisian arcade. There are wrought-iron chairs covered in scarlet and gold cushions, small trees in giant urns, and a big band tinkling in the background. It's like a miniature (but much more intimate) version of the Great Court at the British Museum.

Like the eclectic museum collection, the long menu of seasonal French dishes is rather hit and miss. Brasserie classics such as steak tartare, sole meunière and tarte tatin tend to be perfectly acceptable but unexceptional. (Even the afternoon tea has a Gallic twist: it comes with foie gras, goose rillette and a selection of French fancies, although scones with clotted cream are also on offer.) Nevertheless, a good time is a given because the place exudes a great sense of occasion. The best time to visit is for a breakfast treat (try the ham and gruyère omelette) or for a romantic rendezvous on Friday or Saturday evening, when the restaurant stays open for dinner after the museum has closed. The sumptuous setting invites extravagance: it's the kind of place where you can't resist ordering a glass of champagne. Postprandial canoodling is pretty much guaranteed.

PAUL ROTHE & SON

35 Marylebone Lane, Marylebone, W1U 2NN
- 020 7935 6783
- Open Mon–Fri, 8am–6pm, Sat 11.30am–5.30pm, closed Sun
- Transport Marble Arch or Bond Street tube
- Moderate

Tea and sympathy

There's something utterly irresistible about a café with a large sign outside that says: HOT SOUP. At this charming time warp, the soup in question never fails to delight, whether it's creamy leek and potato or spicy Thai chicken. Served in pretty vintage bowls with a crusty buttered roll, the potage is as comforting as the kindly staff, invariably wearing white coats and a smile.

This quaint café, which doubles as a delicatessen, is as much about the people as the superlative produce. Dating back to 1900, it's been in the Rothe family for four generations – ever since the current owner's German grandfather arrived in London on a coal barge. "At the time, it was one of only three delicatessens in London. People would come from all over town for their rye loaves," says Paul Rothe, who has been installed behind the sandwich bar since 1969.

Devoted regulars still come from far and wide for the Ukrainian rye bread. Despite the ongoing chi-chification of Marylebone, Paul Rothe & Son has preserved the old-fashioned charm of the village grocer. Wood-clad walls are lined with traditional treats evocative of children's parties and family picnics – chutneys and pickles, preserves and marmalades, lemon curd, English mustard, peppermint humbugs and Highland fudge.

The eat-in or take-away menu is also a smorgasbord of comfort food for the terminally nostalgic: marmite and cucumber sandwiches, salt beef, mustard and dill pickle baps, a mug of Bovril, a caramel slice. A few exotic items do feature, notably the Austrian *liptauer* (cream cheese with paprika, chives and capers) and *kummelkase* (stilton, caraway seeds and cream cheese) sandwiches.

Order at the counter and take a seat in one of the Formica booths with folding leatherette seats. There's great pleasure to be had from eavesdropping on Rothe & Son's conversations with their customers, who range from despatch riders to besuited businessmen.

"Have we tempted you with anything else?" Rothe asks an elegant octogenarian stocking up on cranberry and pistachio cake.

"I had a different combination altogether today – I'm trying to catch you out," teases one regular, as she pays for her Scotch egg and liver sausage sandwich.

"No tomatoes, please," says a glamorous American, with a wave of her manicured hand.

"But they're very good for you."

"I don't like them."

All in all, a most civilised way to spend an afternoon.

L'ATELIER DES CHEFS

19 Wigmore Street, Marylebone, W1U 1PH
- 020 7499 6580
- www.atelierdeschefs.co.uk
- Open Mon–Sat 10am–7pm. Class times vary – check website for details
- Transport Oxford Circus or Bond Street tube
- Expensive

Making a meal of it

This culinary school provides instant gratification: you can eat what you've cooked as soon as your dishes are ready. There are classes for all abilities: you can squeeze a half-hour session into your lunch break, perfect pasta making in two hours, or take a four-hour master-class in Indian cuisine. I chose a ninety-minute Cook and Dine evening class, with a menu apparently lifted from an Islington gastro-pub: mushroom *velouté*, rump steak with truffled crushed potatoes and creamy Savoy cabbage, followed by sticky toffee pudding with *crème anglaise*.

Eight of us had signed up. My fellow students were a statuesque French woman who had come to master the art of sticky toffee pudding ("I adore British food," she sighed), two young editors from Bloomsbury ("We publish Heston and Hugh so we get to try out all their recipes"), a teenage trainee chef from Leeds with her mum ("This is way more hands-on than catering college - all we ever make is biscuits"), and a couple of law students from Canada (who seemed more interested in eating each other than our three-course dinner).

Donning plastic aprons, we rolled up our sleeves and gathered round chef Louis Solley's spotless stove. Solley, a puckish 20-something with dazzling knife skills and a quick wit, is a natural teacher. He makes everything look simple and puts everyone at ease. "Normally I'm locked in a basement kitchen with nobody to talk to, so I like to give the customers a good grilling."

We started with dessert, the trickiest dish on tonight's menu. We beat the sugar, and butter by hand, instead of in a food processor, avoiding wrist strain as we took turns blending the mixture to golden putty. Tasks are divided to save time, but we all get our hands dirty.

Louis had pre-prepared a wild mushroom stock for the soup. He showed us how to finely dice shallots, although it took me five times longer than him. I learned how to smash raw garlic and salt into a smooth paste, and discovered that you should only slice parsley once or it will go bitter. The men relish the job of searing the steaks over a smoking pan. The table is laid while we're clumsily piping goat's cheese and crème fraiche onto warm croutons.

We ate each course together, oohing and aahing over the results. Louis tells us his cholesterol is 8.5; after devouring three courses in which butter and cream are the star ingredients, I can see why. But every bite was worth it.

POSTCARD TEAS

9 Dering Street, Mayfair, W1S 1AG
• 020 7629 3654
• www.postcardteas.com
• Open Mon—Sat 10.30am—6.30pm
• Transport Bond Street or Oxford Circus tube
• Moderate

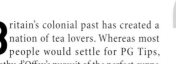

Just add water

Britain's colonial past has created a nation of tea lovers. Whereas most people would settle for PG Tips, Timothy d'Offay's pursuit of the perfect cuppa has taken him all over India and the Far East. At Postcard Teas, connoisseurs can sample his signature blends and single-estate teas from India, Sri Lanka, China, Japan, Taiwan, Korea and Vietnam.

The loose-leaf tea is sold in elegant caddies decorated with vintage postcards from Tim's personal collection. Alternatively, vacuum-packed pouches of chai and oolong can be posted directly to fellow tea fanatics worldwide from the shop's own red letterbox. A postmark shows the tea's provenance, including the estate and region where it was produced. It's not your typical mail order – but this is not your typical teashop.

Tea was first sold here 200 years ago when this was a grocery store; the original 18th-century frontage is intact. The spare interior offers a welcome respite from the bling of Bond Street. A pared-down Japanese aesthetic and barely audible classical music create a cocoon of calm, even when it's busy. "The shop was born out of the frustration of buying expensive tea from food halls, but not being able to taste or even smell it," says Tim, as he brews me a cup of Master Matsumoto's "Supernatural" tea – it won't give you super-powers, but it's absolutely pesticide and fertiliser free. The shop also stocks delightful tea paraphernalia such as patchwork tea cosies from India and tin caddies hand-made in Kyoto.

All the teas can be tried at the communal tasting table, each one served in a different cup, beaker or saucer that reflects its roots. The rarest teas are made from ancient plants using ancestral techniques. Master Luo's green tea comes from the same 18 bushes reserved for the Chinese President since the 18th century. Master Liu makes Pu-erh tea that dates back to the time of Gengis Khan.

The menu contains tasting notes – "a sweet soft *sencha* with lots of *umami*", "a mild grassy green tea with a citrus finish" – that might sound pretentious. Postcard Teas is aimed at purists, yet it's surprisingly accessible. Come alone and savour a delicate cup of tea and a delicious moment of solitude – a restorative ritual worth repeating every day. But remember: there's no toilet, so don't drink too much.

COURTHOUSE HOTEL BAR

Courthouse Doubletree Hotel, 19–21 Great Marlborough Street, Soho,
W1F 7HL
- 020 7297 5555
- www.courthouse-hotel.com
- Open Mon–Sat 11am–1.30am, Sun 11am–11pm
- Transport Oxford Circus tube
- Moderate

Jailhouse Rock

"**G**oing to prison is my greatest fear," confides Carly Lipman, events manager at Soho's Courthouse Hotel. Lipman's professionalism is admirable: we are huddled in a cramped prison cell clad in white tiles, with a urinal in the corner and a heavy steel door. It's not somewhere I'd like to be locked up either – the tiny room has all the charm of a public toilet. It's one of three holding cells converted into private drinking areas as part of the transformation of Great Marlborough Street Magistrates Court into a Doubletree Hilton hotel in 2005.

Six people can fit in each cell, but thankfully the door always stays open now. "In the past, some drinkers got out of hand behind closed doors," Carly explains, as we browse the criminally themed cocktails (Behind Bars, Thieving Daiquiri, Inmates Bramble), served with spring rolls and seafood platters that are a step up from standard prison fare. Not much has been done to spruce up the interior, though: the only mod cons are some plastic cushions on the coffin-sized bed, a glass coffee table, and two squat stools wrapped in denim that look like the cut-off midriffs of the oversized American tourists who populate the hotel.

The decor might be drab but the history of these cells is certainly colourful. Mick Jagger, Johnny Rotten, Francis Bacon and Bob Marley all spent a night here after being busted with drugs. The worst offender was Keith Richards: in 1973, he was fined £205 for possession of marijuana, heroin, mandrax, an unlicensed revolver and an antique shotgun.

Formerly a court and police station, Great Marlborough Street was the second oldest magistrates' court in Britain, dating back to the 1800s. The oak-panelled Number One court has been turned into an Asian restaurant, with some Buddhas perched uncomfortably above the original dock, witness stand and judge's bench. Charles Dickens covered many criminal trials in this room as a reporter for the *Morning Chronicle*. It's also where Oscar Wilde accused the Marquess of Queensbury of libel in 1895, after Queensbury called him a "posing somdomite" [sic]. It was a foolish move by Wilde, who was having an affair with Queensbury's son Douglas: the details of Wilde's salacious sex life that surfaced in the trial forced him to drop the charges – and ultimately led to Wilde's imprisonment, bankruptcy and demise.

INAMO

134 Wardour Street, Soho, W1F 8ZP
- 020 7851 7051 • www.inamo-restaurant.com
- Also at 4–12 Lower Regent Street, St James, SW1Y 4PE
- 0207 484 0500 • www.inamo-stjames.com
- Open Soho: Mon–Thu noon–3pm, 5–11.30pm, Fri–Sat noon–midnight, Sun noon–10.30pm; St James: noon–12.30am daily
- Transport Leicester Square or Piccadilly Circus tube
- Moderate

Geek chic

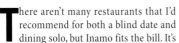

There aren't many restaurants that I'd recommend for both a blind date and dining solo, but Inamo fits the bill. It's what Hollywood producers would dub "high concept". That concept might be summed up as "interactive Manga comic for gourmet geeks".

Twenty-somethings Noel Hunwick and Danny Potter were barely out of university when they dreamed up the notion of a restaurant with touch-screen menus where you could order a beer or get the bill at the touch of a button. The idea developed over dinner, as they struggled to attract an elusive waiter's attention. Instead of complaining or leaving a measly tip, as most disgruntled diners would, Noel and Danny responded by creating "the world's first interactive ordering system that uses overhead projection technology to give the customer complete control over their dining experience".

If this sounds off-putting, don't be alarmed. Even technophobes should have little trouble with the interactive menus beamed onto the tabletops at Inamo. Click on pictures of pan-Asian dishes and they're brought to your table in quick succession. Unlike conveyer belt sushi bars where the food always tastes a little stale, everything is made to order. In keeping with the interactive shtick, there are lots of little dishes designed for sharing: delicious grilled eel and avocado *maki*, slivers of sea bass marinated in kelp, a parcel of sake salmon wrapped in cedarwood. Pork neck with confit of apple and spicy chocolate sauce melts in the mouth. The presentation is always pretty, but portions are small so the price will creep up. Set lunches and pre-theatre bento boxes are better value.

There are plenty of high-tech features to entertain solitary diners or awkward dates. You can customise your virtual tablecloth (good for frustrated creatives), spy on the kitchen using the Chef Cam (reassuring for hygiene freaks), scroll through tips on local highlights (handy for tourists), or order a cab (a godsend on a dodgy date).

There are two branches of Inamo (which doesn't actually mean anything in Japanese, but is supposed to be evocative of both "enamour" and "in a moment"). The original Soho venue is smaller and darker. The Regent Street branch is glossier, with a bamboo forest and a backlit onyx bar where the brave knock back Inamo martinis with chilli, mandarin and spring onion. A safer bet is the Bloody Geisha, a blend of vodka and *shochu* spiced with soy tomato juice.

CENTRE POINT SUSHI CAFÉ

20–21 St Giles High Street, WC2H 8LH
- 020 7240 6147
- www.cpfs.co.uk
- Open Mon–Fri noon–3pm, 6–11pm
- Transport Tottenham Court Road tube
- Moderate

> **Superlative
> sushi above
> a supermarket**

There's something perversely appealing about a restaurant that refuses to publicise itself and treats reviewers with contempt. Such is the Centre Point Sushi Café, also known as Hana Sushi. This unassuming joint is located in a Korean enclave behind Centre Point, probably London's ugliest landmark.

Admittedly, the view from Paramount (the exclusive members' club on Centre Point's top floor) is astonishing, and Renzo Piano's Central St Giles is a welcome injection of primary colour to the area; but no amount of PR puff can tart up this grubby little corner of north west, north, north east & east. Perhaps that will change with the new Crossrail train station at Tottenham Court Road, opening in 2018. Until then, sushi lovers can only hope that gentrification is kept at bay.

Across the road from the fantastic Korean canteens along St Giles High Street, where tiny fashion students gobble huge bowls of *bibimbap*, is the Centre Point Food Store. This Korean/Japanese supermarket has some of the surliest staff you will ever encounter. Pay no attention, and instead make your way upstairs to the small restaurant. With its leatherette booths and scuffed sushi counter, the dining room feels authentic and relaxed. Although it looks as if it's been around since the 70s, apparently it opened in 2005. (It's hard to get the facts straight, as the waiters speak almost no English and nod enthusiastically whatever you say.)

The menu is traditional: no frills, no fusion – just Japanese classics at decent prices. When dining alone, I like to sit at the counter and sample a selection of *maki* and *sashimi*, expertly rolled and sliced by the laconic Japanese chef. Eel *nigiri*, soft-shell crab and scallops are all exceptionally good. One or two daily specials are scrawled in marker pen on a board. The bento boxes and set lunches are good value, and usually come with *miso* soup, pickles and fresh fruit. If you're with company, try to bag a window booth overlooking Centre Point – it looks much prettier after dark, when all the lights are on.

If you can stomach the gruff service downstairs, pick up some *nori*, rice crackers and gummy bears from the supermarket on your way out.

THE PHOENIX ARTIST CLUB

1 Phoenix Street, Covent Garden, WC2H 0DT
- 020 7836 1077
- www.phoenixartistclub.com
- Open Mon–Sat 5pm–2am
- Admission Members only after 8pm; no admission after 1am. Free for members' guests
- Transport Leicester Square or Tottenham Court Road tube
- Moderate

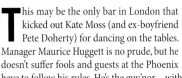

Actors anonymous

This may be the only bar in London that kicked out Kate Moss (and ex-boyfriend Pete Doherty) for dancing on the tables. Manager Maurice Huggett is no prude, but he doesn't suffer fools and guests at the Phoenix have to follow his rules. He's the guv'nor – with a hefty dose of high camp.

Fond of flamboyant waistcoats, Huggett has run this eccentric members' club for actors and entertainers (which he calls "my living room") since 2000. But the former dressing rooms of the Phoenix Theatre were first converted into a wine bar in the late 70s by a long-forgotten Italian couple. Most of the original decor remains unchanged: stained-glass screens depicting London theatres, ornate ceiling tiles, portraits of old music-hall stars, and a fetching painting of a teenage Sophia Loren. More recent additions include masks and props, signed photos of soap stars and posters from musicals – a tribute to the club's theatrical clientele.

Equity members get discounted rates and if you're working in a West End show, you get complimentary membership for a year. Affordable and unstuffy, the Phoenix is the antithesis of Soho's snooty members' clubs. It's not glamorous, just good fun. The bartender knows all the regulars and most of them seem to know each other. The music, mainly show tunes and soundtracks, isn't so loud that you can't have a conversation; although occasionally you might stumble on an impromptu sing-along with Charlotte Church, or an octogenarian pianist pounding out jazz standards.

Huggett's predecessor, John Shuttleworth, ran a restaurant called Shuttleworth's here (better known as Shut's because of its erratic opening hours). Perhaps not surprisingly, he went bankrupt. These days, the Phoenix is one of the few places in London where you can always get a drink after hours. "When I open the doors, I never know who'll walk in," says Huggett. "From student actors to stars, peers of the realm to politicians, members of the royal family and royal forces, everyone comes here – except the paparazzi."

It's no longer strictly a members' bar, now that the licensing laws have been relaxed, but the door policy prevents overcrowding and filters out the riff-raff. Full of hard-drinking luvvies, it's not for the faint-hearted. In the words of one regular, inscribed by the entrance: "No-one with any vestige of fear or scruple should venture into this terrifying club."

ROSSO DI SERA

5 Monmouth Street, Covent Garden, WC2H 9DA
- 020 7240 3683
- www.sibillafoods.com
- Open Food served Mon–Thurs noon–3pm & 6–11pm, Fri–Sat noon–11.30pm, Sun noon–11pm. The café is open from 10am-5pm.
- Transport Covent Garden or Tottenham Court Road tube
- Moderate

Excellent Restaurant Downstairs

This is one of those inconspicuous places you could walk past dozens of times and never think to enter. At street level, Rosso di Sera looks like a slightly shabby sandwich bar that happens to do proper Italian coffee. But follow the sign to the "Excellent Restaurant Downstairs" and you won't be disappointed. In the basement is a brilliant trattoria that specialises in food and wines from Le Marche. Lodged between the Adriatic sea and the Apennine mountains, this unsung region of central Italy has somehow escaped the Disneyfication of other parts of the country. One besotted Bloomberg journalist described Le Marche's cuisine thus: "Fried olives, creamy prosciuttos, depraved lasagnes".

You can sample all these, and many more, regional delicacies here. Owners Igor Iacopini and Samuele Ciaralli have known each other since they were five. As schoolboys, they shared a dream: to play football for Ancona. Today, they have "switched their focus from footballs to meatballs". They spent eight months visiting artisanal producers in Le Marche, sourcing ingredients that aren't available anywhere else in Britain. They travel home every few months to replenish their supplies of *salame di Fabriano*, *prosciutto di Carpegna*, and *pecorino* matured in grape must. These appear on the restaurant's unmissable cured meat and cheese platters, served on olive-wood boards and accompanied with dollops of grape must, wild berry jam and chestnut honey.

Everything else, from tagliatelle ragu to tiramisu, is created by a single chef in the tiny kitchen. You might have to wait, but it's worth it. The set lunch menu is incredible value, but do try traditional dishes such as the curiously moreish *olive all' Ascolana* (deep-fried green olives stuffed with meat), *vincisgrassi* (a killer lasagne made with veal, pork and chicken giblets), and *vino cotto con biscotti secchi* (described as "dry cookies served with boiled wine"– much tastier than it sounds). Fresh pasta is made daily but only used in some dishes, so ask before you order. There are dozens of wines from Le Marche – the region has 18 different grape varieties – as well as craft beers.

All the staff are Italian, as are most of the customers. "Our patrons from Le Marche say it's just like eating in their country house," says Igor. Half a dozen tables are squeezed into the ochre room. The exposed bricks and beams were salvaged from Igor's father's house. On your way out, stock up on products from the ground floor deli, and gloat as you watch the office workers chomping their panini, unaware of what they're missing downstairs.

POETRY CAFÉ

22 Betterton Street, Covent Garden, WC2H 9BX
- 020 7420 9887
- www.poetrysociety.org.uk/content/cafe/
- Open Mon–Fri noon–11pm; Sat 7–11pm; closed Sun
- Transport Covent Garden or Holborn tube
- Budget

Well versed

There's nothing glamorous or trendy about the Poetry Café, housed in the same building as The Poetry Society, founded in 1909 to promote the study and enjoyment of British verse. Unlike so many arts or academic institutions, it's neither self-important nor inaccessible. Like the brilliant "Poems on the Underground" initiative, the Poetry Café introduces a moment of quiet contemplation into the clutter and clamour of everyday life in London.

A haven from the West End hubbub in the backstreets of Covent Garden, the narrow, sparely furnished café is rarely busy during the day. There's usually the odd writer scrawling into a journal, poring over the small library of literary reviews and second-hand poetry volumes, or simply lost in thought. The staff will leave you in peace and let you linger as long as you like. The vegetarian food is pretty good, too. The daily menu is short but wholesome: typically, it might be Greek salad, lentil and coconut soup, spinach quiche, and pasta with walnuts, broccoli and gruyère. Cakes are made on the premises and the bread and cheese are from Neal's Yard.

In the evenings, things liven up as the focus shifts to the poetry readings that take place in the basement. The room may be stuffy and somewhat shabby, but the atmosphere is intimate, supportive and sociable. There are events nearly every night (except Sundays), including regular open mic nights, book launches, and occasionally live music or screenings to accompany the verse. There's no need to book tickets in advance, but it's worth checking what's on before you go (www.poetrysociety.org.uk/events/calendar).

NEARBY

AMPHITHEATRE RESTAURANT
(Royal Opera House, Bow Street, WC2B; 020 7240 1200 or 020 7212 9254; www.roh.org.uk)
In the evenings, this swish restaurant on the top floor of the Royal Opera House is only open to ticket holders. At lunchtime, anyone can enjoy British comfort food with marvellous views of Covent Garden's market and across the rooftops to Nelson's Column. It's especially lovely on summer afternoons, when tables are set on a secret terrace.

LE BEAUJOLAIS

25 Litchfield Street, Covent Garden, WC2H 9NJ
- 020 7836 2955
- Open Mon—Fri noon—11pm, Sat 5—11pm, closed Sun
- Transport Leicester Square or Covent Garden tube
- Moderate

*Grape
expectations*

It's not just the name that's a giveaway. You know you've entered a shrine to the Gamay grape the moment you enter this wine bar. You have to squeeze past giant placards of different grape varieties just to get in. There are wine labels stuck to the lampshades and wine crates glued to the bar. Bizarrely, there are also hundreds of beer tankards dangling from the ceiling, along with dozens of ties belonging to denizens of the members-only restaurant in the basement next door.

"The place is of course older than I am," smiles Pascal Perry, the grey-haired, flush-cheeked patron installed behind the bar for over 30 years. Perry claims this was the first French wine bar in London. It opened in the 1960s as Winkles, but became "really French" in the 70s when Perry's predecessor Joel took over. It was Joel who started the tradition of confiscating customers' ties when they loosened up after a few drinks.

"Everything in this establishment is French except two things – my customers and my music," says Perry. He has a penchant for rock and blues, thankfully played at low volume. The Arsenal football merchandise doesn't look terribly French either, but there's no mistaking the provenance of the staff, whose accents are as creamy as ripe camembert. They know all the regulars (including many of their expat compatriots) by name.

Like the lived-in decor - a clutter of Gallic knick-knacks – the short menu never changes. It's rustic fare: pâté, rillettes, *boeuf bourguignon*, Toulouse sausages and a suitably stinky cheeseboard. The exclusively French wine list includes every Beaujolais appellation. Most are reasonably priced, but be prepared to take the rough with the smooth. Inevitably, it gets rammed when the Beaujolais Nouveau is released on the third Thursday of November. A special game-based lunch is served in the members' club, but gets booked up months in advance. To join the club, you must be recommended by a member or put in plenty of drinking hours at the bar.

Miraculously, the tourists swarming the West End always bypass this hideaway. Dark, cosy, occasionally loud, and consistently welcoming, Le Beaujolais warms the heart on a chilly winter's evening. Just a few doors down from The Ivy, it couldn't be less pretentious.

NEARBY

VISTA
(2 Spring Gardens, Trafalgar Square, SW1A 2TS, www.thetrafalgar.com)
A summer sanctuary from the West End hordes, the rooftop bar at the Trafalgar Hotel has sensational city views, almost eye level with Nelson's Column and the London Eye.

SOHO'S SECRET TEA ROOM

Above the Coach & Horses, 29 Greek Street, Soho, W1D 5DH
- 020 7437 5920
- www.sohossecrettearoom.co.uk
- Open noon–8pm daily; closed every other Wed afternoon for Private Eye lunch
- Transport Leicester Square, Tottenham Court Road or Piccadilly Circus tube
- Moderate

A slice of cake and Soho history

Only a very special cake shop could lure me away from Maison Bertaux, the heavenly Greek Street patisserie that has kept resting actors in raspberry tarts since 1871. Next door is another Soho institution: the Coach & Horses, still known as Norman's among die-hard regulars. Norman Balon, who crowned himself "London's rudest landlord", ran the Coach from 1943 until 2006. "I don't care whether you're a man or a woman, you can go now," he'd bark at boorish patrons. "Italians and shoplifters" drank at the Greek Street or "shallow end". Hard-drinking artists and hacks, including Francis Bacon, Lucian Freud and Dylan Thomas, drank at the Romilly Street or "deep end". Jeffrey Bernard, whose *Spectator* column "Low Life" summed up life at the Coach, was immortalised by Peter O'Toole in Keith Waterhouse's play *Jeffrey Bernard is Unwell*; the set was a meticulous reconstruction of the pub's nicotine-stained interior.

Thankfully the charming new landlord, Alastair Choat, has barely altered the decor, with its wood-lined walls, battered bar stools and frosted windows to block out the fact that it's only noon and you're nursing a double Scotch. They serve Scotch eggs and sausage rolls, although most regulars believe "eating is cheating". Not so the staff of *Private Eye*, who have held their fortnightly lunches in a room upstairs for 47 years.

You have to sneak behind the bar to access the dining room, which Choat has converted into a delightful tearoom, putting his vast collection of vintage china, embroidered linens and 78 records to good use. A gramophone spins 1940s' swing while sweet waitresses in pinafores serve afternoon tea: warm scones with home-made jam and clotted cream, a wedge of lemon drizzle or Victoria sponge cake, and cucumber, egg and cress or smoked salmon and cream cheese sandwiches (crusts off, of course). There's a connoisseur's selection of loose-leaf teas, from rosebud to jasmine pearl. Many customers come in period attire; you might get a free glass of champagne if you dress the part.

BY THE SAME LANDLORD

SMITHFIELD'S SECRET TEA ROOM

(105 Charterhouse Street, EC1M 6HR; 020 7253 3882)
Soho's sister tearoom in Smithfield is even cosier and more clandestine. Opening hours are erratic, so call ahead or ring the bell by the brown door beside the Smithfield Tavern and try your luck. A carpeted staircase leads to a secret salon that could be your great aunt's parlour.

NEW EVARISTO CLUB

57 Greek Street, Soho, W1D 3DX
• 020 7437 9536
• Open 5.30pm–1am daily
• Transport Leicester Square or Tottenham Court Road tube
• Budget

> *Old-school Soho hideout*

There aren't many members' clubs in Soho that are accessible to pretty much anyone, but this unpretentious dive is an exception. There's none of the exclusive veneer of celebrity haunts such as Soho House or The Groucho, and the basement bar is so small that there's no room for oversized egos.

It's not immediately obvious that there's a bar here at all. The entrance is through an unmarked door in a grotty building (the kind that normally advertises "Models Upstairs"). Look for the buzzer that says "Trisha/Evaristo Club". Although officially called the New Evaristo Club, most regulars know it as Trisha's (after the owner, Trisha Bergonzi), or as The Hideout. On weekends there's usually a doorman loitering outside, who can generally be sweet-talked into letting you in even if you're not a member. Sometimes they'll make you sign the guestbook and charge you a pound or two on the door; sometimes they'll just wave you through.

A sticky carpet leads downstairs to a room that's straight out of a 1960s' mafia job. The walls are half-lined with mock-chalet wood panelling. The rest of the space is plastered in lime-green paint, photos of boxers, favoured patrons and Italian legends such as Frank Sinatra, Don Corleone and the Pope. There are a few rickety chairs and tables, and a small Formica bar from which the gnarled bar staff dispense cheap wine, warm beer and witty asides.

Arrive early or very late on weekends. After the surrounding pubs close, an assortment of random characters piles in – transvestites, hipsters, fashion students and elderly Italians who have long called this corner of Soho home. The occasional celebrity makes an appearance, but nobody seems to notice. If you're lucky, a jazz crooner or rock and roll band will squeeze into the corner and start jamming. There's no dance-floor but that doesn't stop the crowd from going wild.

There's a single scruffy toilet and a tiny smoking area at the back where you're bound to make friends, if not make out with someone. Anything goes.

NEARBY

ALGERIAN COFFEE STORES
(52 Old Compton Street, Soho, W1D 4PB; 020 7437 2480, www.algcoffee.co.uk)
Founded in 1887, this classic coffee emporium has preserved much of its stunning Victorian interior. As well as over 80 types of coffee, 120 teas, and all sorts of sweet treats to take home, they serve perhaps the finest – and certainly the cheapest – espresso and cappuccino in London at the worn wooden counter.

BOBBY'S BAR

1 Upper St James Street, Soho, W1F 9DF
• 020 3145 1000
• www.bobbobricard.com
• Open Tues–Sat 6pm–12.30am
• Transport Oxford Circus or Piccadilly Circus tube
• Expensive

> *Subterranean opulence*

I'm a sucker for a good booth. Bob Bob Ricard, which bills itself as a "diner-deluxe", is a glorious roomful of cobalt leather booths offset by clashing Art Deco wallpaper. Designed by David Collins, it's like a souped-up 1930s' ocean liner with a dash of the Orient Express. There's a mottled marble bar where you can get sozzled on pink rhubarb gin and tonics alongside Soho's film execs.

If you're more partial to vodka and would rather not see and be seen, head down to the hidden basement bar. It's like a set from *Mad Men*, down to the pianist playing Sinatra tunes on a baby grand most nights. You can picture Don Draper seducing his latest squeeze in one of the tall red leather booths. (They're a tight fit, which adds to the intimate atmosphere.) Expertly mixed cocktails focus on British ingredients such as the BBR Botanical (Pimm's, Hendrick's gin, elderflower, sparkling wine).

Such opulence doesn't come cheap, but mark-ups on fine wines and champagnes are relatively modest, with margins capped at £50 per bottle. Top-class vodkas, all served at –18 degrees, are hand-picked by one of the two owners, Bob, who hails from Russia (and is actually called Leonid Shutov). "Bob" recommends the Kauffman 2006 vodka with a hint of honey. After one too many dirty martinis, resist the urge to order caviar and blinis (unless Draper is paying). Matchstick chips and flaky tartlets with sophisticated toppings such as fig, honey and mascarpone will hit the spot.

Bobby's Bar is never oversubscribed and you won't have to fight to get to the bar, as standing room isn't allowed. You can book in advance, but with 80 covers and a secretive door policy that relies on word of mouth, that probably won't be necessary. Premium cocktails, proper booths, and a glamorous sanctuary from the Soho scrum: what more could you want?

CHAMPAGNE ON CALL

In the main restaurant upstairs every booth has a champagne button so you can summon more bubbly in the twinkling of an eye. The house champagne is Pol Roger, Winston Churchill's favourite. As he once said of his preferred tipple: "In victory, deserve it; in defeat, need it."

EXPERIMENTAL COCKTAIL CLUB

13A Gerrard Street, Chinatown, W1D 5PS
- 020 7434 3559
- www.chinatownecc.com
- Open Mon–Sat 6pm–3am, Sun 6pm–midnight. For reservations call 07825 215 877 or email reservation@chinatownecc.com before 5pm Tues–Sat
- Transport Leicester Square or Piccadilly Circus tube
- Expensive (cover charge after 11pm)

Chinesey speakeasy

Very few Londoners I know would admit to eating out in Chinatown. For me, it's a flashback to slimy noodles served by the world's surliest waiters after drunken nights out as a student. Today, no amount of alcohol could tempt me back into the neon-bright restaurants that line Gerrard Street. But you could twist my arm with the prospect of a decent cocktail.

Lurking among the roast ducks strung up by their necks is a secret speakeasy. Look for the scratched black door opposite Top of the Town restaurant. There's no sign and no sign of life during the day. But as night falls, two bouncers appear outside. If you're smart enough to have made a reservation or just look sharp enough, they'll usher you into a dusky stairwell. Upstairs, you're transported

to 1930s Shanghai: chinoiserie wallpaper, mirrored ceilings, leopard-print carpets, and low velvet love seats for snuggling up to your date. Candles flicker in crystal tumblers. Heavy drapes block out the bright lights and greasy aromas of Gerrard Street. Spread over two floors, it's already buzzing at 7pm. Cocktail shakers rattle over the jazzy soundtrack like a percussion section.

The Experimental Cocktail Club takes its name a little too literally. The mixologist seems to have a wilful obsession with obscure ingredients – ever heard of Cynar, Batavia Arrack or Velvet Falernum? Eventually, we settled for a Drunken Viking – a glorified cucumber and grapefruit martini topped up with soda. The lurid orange Rendez Vous (Hendrick's Gin, Aperol, Noilly Pratt, rhubarb syrup, lemon juice and a pinch of Himalayan purple salt) tasted like one of those medicinal sachets you force down when you feel the flu coming on. Our glamorous waitress didn't offer us a refund, but suggested we try the St-Germain-des-Prés instead. The catalogue of ingredients (Plymouth gin, St-Germain liqueur, lime juice, elderflower cordial, egg white, spiced tincture and cucumber juice) didn't convince us. At least we didn't blow the budget on a "vintage cocktail", which start at £120 a pop.

The French owners, Olivier Bon, Pierre-Charles Cros and Romée de Gorianoff, already have three successful bars in Paris. They've scored another hit here, judging by the animated throng of scene-setters soaking up the sultry ambience. There's live music every Tuesday night, classical music and complimentary massages on Sundays. Some customers are even brave enough to sample the Chinese restaurants on their way home.

UPSTAIRS AT RULES

35 Maiden Lane, Covent Garden, WC2E 7LB
• 020 7836 5314
• www.rules.co.uk
• Open Mon–Sat noon–11.30pm, Sun noon–10.30pm
• Transport Covent Garden or Charing Cross tube
• Expensive

Rules worth following

"I hate rules", my drinking companion opined. But he looked extremely pleased with himself as he drained his Screaming Viking.

Upstairs at Rules is my idea of the perfect cocktail bar. Hidden above London's oldest restaurant (est. 1798), this sumptuous hideaway was once a private dining room, where Edward VII canoodled with his paramour, Lillie Langtry. It's still a great venue for a clandestine date. Never advertised and rarely crowded, it's like having access to a gentlemen's club, without the fusty chauvinism or complicated door policy. All royal portraits, antlers and wood panelling, it's the kind of place where you can bring your lover, your mother or your boss.

Another great thing about this quintessentially British institution is the American-style service. Reserve a stool at the bar so you can get an eyeful of Bostonian bartender Brian Silva in action. Formerly at The Connaught and Scott's, Brian frowns on fruity flourishes and fancy garnishes (apart from the odd infusion of violet or rose petal). He serves classic cocktails inspired by the 1930s that feature his collection of rare spirits, including 42 vermouths. Most are stirred, not shaken. Brian will happily whip up a bespoke cocktail, based on your favourite tipple. But one of the ten signature cocktails – as dry as the wit who named them – is sure to tickle your fancy: perhaps Chorus Girl No 5, le Blonde, or my current favourite, Swedish Diplomat (Venezuelan Diplomatico rum, Swedish punch, and a squeeze of lime poured around a crystal ball of solid ice that melts ever so slowly, allowing the punchy spice to subtly infuse the drink.)

Rules doesn't do music, beer, coffee or tea. But it does serve divine bar snacks like quail Scotch eggs and Cornish crab paté from noon until 5pm, as well as complimentary caramelised nuts and wedges of stilton.

After his second Screaming Viking, my companion became fixated with the swirly scarlet and gold carpet. I was more intent on finding the fox hidden in the hunting frieze (salvaged from The Savoy during a recent makeover). Owner John Mayhew had himself, his dogs and his 1935 Rolls Royce "Bubbles" painted into the scene, which could just as well be Lartington, Mayhew's country estate, which provides all the game for Rules. On shoot days, you must try the Buckshot Bullshot, Brian's twist on a Bloody Mary made with a shot of beef consommé.

Brian is usually on duty Monday to Friday. Take my advice and treat yourself to a cocktail in his company on a dreary midweek afternoon. Just the sight of that gold "Reserved" sign on the gleaming bar is guaranteed to lift your spirits.

CELLARDOOR

Zero Aldwych, Covent Garden, WC2E 7DN
- 020 7240 8848
- www.cellardoor.biz
- Open 4pm–1am daily; live performances start around 9pm
- Transport Temple, Covent Garden or Charing Cross tube
- Moderate (no cover charge, but a 10% "late and live" charge is added to your bill after 9pm)

Louche loos

"I ran May Balls at University, went to the occasional lecture and wrote the odd essay. Thirty years later, I'm still doing exactly the same thing," says Paul Kohler, who clearly relishes his double life as a club owner and law professor.

Kohler's underground bar takes its WC postcode very literally. Formerly the Wellington Street Gents, this public convenience was allegedly frequented by celebrity cruisers Oscar Wilde, John Gielgud and John Hurt. "I'd walked past this disused public toilet every day for years – a prime space in the heart of London – and just thought: why not?" Kohler recalls.

Kohler persuaded Westminster Council to grant him a late licence as long as he staged live entertainment. Since the tiny space only holds 60 people, Kohler plumped for cabaret, which comes from the Dutch word "*camberete*", meaning "small room". Every night is different, from burlesque shows to drag DJs, saucy comedy acts to singers belting out tunes from the Weimar Republic. Many unsigned acts can claim to have made their West End debut at Tuesdays' open mic night. Unlike the surrounding theatres, there's no cover charge and even the popcorn is free.

The street-level entrance looks like a futuristic version of the Paris Metro. Downstairs, walls of angled mirrors and coloured spotlights create the illusion of space. The minute stage, surrounded by scarlet and black banquettes, is concealed by velvet drapes. They've even managed to squeeze in a piano and a dance floor. You have to edge past the performers to get to the toilets, which are designed to titillate. The transparent glass doors become opaque when you lock them. "It's great," says Kohler. "People never leave the loos in a mess when they know you can see inside."

Both glamorous and faintly sleazy, this is something of a pick-up joint. The text message jukebox is a clever icebreaker for courting couples. There always seem to be a few businessmen buying drinks for pretty young things. It's hard to resist wittily named cocktails like Starbucks Must Die (cognac, Kahlua, vanilla-infused vodka, and a shot of espresso) or my favourite, Honey (I drank the) Daiquiri. And this is probably the only place in London where you can do lines on the bar and nobody will bat an eyelid. They sell snuff in all manner of strange flavours from apricot to absinthe, champagne to Red Bull.

INDIA CLUB

143 Strand, Aldwych, WC2R 1JA
- 020 7836 0650
- www.strand-continental.co.uk
- Open noon–2.30pm, 6–10.50pm daily
- Transport Temple, Covent Garden, Embankment or Charing Cross tube
- Budget (no credit cards)

A colonial curry house

V.K. Krishna Menon, independent India's first High Commissioner in Britain, allegedly drank 50 cups of tea every day. When Menon moved into India House on Aldwych in 1947, he set up the India Club (across the road on the Strand) as somewhere for expats and diplomats to chew the fat over chai after office hours. With founding members including Jawaharlal Nehru and Lady Edwina Mountbatten, the India Club was a hotbed of political activity – and maybe more, as the two allegedly had an affair.

The India Club has survived intact, hidden up a flight of grubby linoleum stairs in the Strand Continental Hotel. (Don't be fooled by the name –it's a hostel with bargain bedrooms overlooking the Thames.) With its cracked leather armchairs, the lounge has been preserved in aspic. It has definitely seen better days. But there's a certain allure to a bar that makes no concession to coolness and plays Ravi Shankar cassettes on a loop. It's still occasionally frequented by the octogenarian members of the Calcutta Rowing Club.

Most patrons pick up some Cobra beers or bring their own booze (there's no corkage charge) and head upstairs to the delightful dining room. With its dark wooden chairs with padded leather seats and portraits of Gandhi, it has the feel of a refectory in a provincial Indian university; in fact, most customers are students and professors from King's College and the LSE, or barristers from the Inns of Court nearby.

In 1957, Menon delivered an eight-hour speech defending India's stand on Kashmir – the longest oration ever delivered at the United Nations. The laconic waiters are less verbose. Dressed in white jackets, they look as though they've been there forever – and most have indeed been around for decades. Gyanaprakasam Joseph, head waiter for 37 years, was such an institution that his obituary was published in *The Guardian*.

The chef has also been here for almost 30 years. The menu still reflects Menon's roots in Kerala, featuring many southern Indian dishes such as *sambar* (tamarind-infused lentil curry), *masala dosa* (crispy pancakes with coconut chutney) and *dahi vada* (lentil dumplings in spicy yoghurt sauce). It's simple home-style cooking, refreshingly free from the lashings of ghee used in so many British curry houses. The lamb *bhuna* and *mughlai* chicken are very good, but only the brave should try the whole chilli *bhajas*. The set menus (vegetarian, meat, or prawn) are a steal.

KNIGHT'S BAR

Simpson's-in-the-Strand, 100 Strand, Aldwych, WC2R 0EW
• 020 7836 9112
• www.simpsonsinthestrand.co.uk
• Open Mon–Sat 11am–11pm, Sun noon–9pm
• Transport Temple, Charing Cross or Embankment tube
• Expensive

Grand
Master

Simpson's-in-the-Strand is one of those venerable London institutions that regulars prefer to keep to themselves. Unlike its stablemate The Savoy, which recently had an unfortunate facelift, Simpson's has aged gracefully. Fashionable haunts such as The Wolseley and The Delaunay may offer a pseudo slice of old-world refinement, but Simpson's is the real deal. While those young pretenders trade in Viennese exoticism, Simpson's is resolutely British. Back in 1862, Master Cook Thomas Davey insisted that everything served in the restaurant must be British. (He even replaced the "menu" with a "bill of fare".) This tradition continues, with native delights such as oxtail faggot with pease pudding, steak and kidney pie, and a turbo-charged English breakfast dubbed The Ten Deadly Sins.

The pièce de resistance is the roast rib of Scottish beef, carved at table by liveried waiters from silver-domed trolleys. This practice began during

Simpson's original incarnation as a chess club: the meat was wheeled out to avoid disturbing the players' concentration. The original booths, or divans, that line one wall of the glorious Edwardian dining room were reserved for chess players. Chess matches were played against other coffee houses, with top-hatted runners carrying news of each move between venues. A chess set is still available, but nowadays diners discussing "fish" are more likely to be talking about the Dover sole than a feeble opponent.

The aroma of roast beef follows you upstairs to the Knight's Bar, an Art Deco hideaway overlooking The Strand. With its gold and black chequerboard bar, squishy leather armchairs and velvet settees burnished by many distinguished bottoms, the bar looks as though it's been here for decades; in fact it opened in 1999. Rarely crowded, it's perfect for pre- or post-theatre drinks without the usual West End crush. The drinks list includes a fine selection of champagnes and all the classics, as well as superlative signature cocktails with punning names such as Divan Intervention and Czech Mate. But the foreign bar snacks – BBQ pork spare ribs, duck spring rolls, spicy chicken wings – would have Davey rolling in his grave.

You can entertain yourself by trying to identify the black and white portraits of famous movie stars, statesmen, boxers and tennis players lining the walls. Many are inscribed to Mr Heck, General Manager of Simpson's from 1919 to 1959. Past patrons include Vincent Van Gogh, Charles Dickens and Charlie Chaplin. George Bernard Shaw was among the diners forced to take shelter in the wine cellar during an air raid in 1917. Shaw left a thank-you note inscribed on the kitchen wall, which survives today.

BERRY BROS & RUDD

3 St James's Street, SW1A 1EG
- 020 7396 9600
- Check www.bbr.com for details of upcoming events
- Shop hours: Mon–Fri 10am–6pm, Sat 10am–5pm; closed Sunday
- Transport Green Park or Piccadilly Circus tube
- Expensive

A lot of bottle

Britain's oldest wine merchants, Berry Bros & Rudd have dispensed rare vintages to bon viveurs since 1698. Still a family business, the shop has barely changed since the Widow Bourne opened The Coffee Mill, selling spices, tea and coffee. The original scales have been used to weigh famous customers (including Lord Byron and Napoleon III) for 300 years. A secret tunnel, now blocked, linked the warren of cellars to St James' Palace, so royals could pay clandestine visits to the ladies of the night who frequented the shop. The shops cellars hold 100,000 bottles, but patrons' finest vintages - worth a staggering £650 million – are laid down in a warehouse in less romantic Basingstoke.

Today, the cellars are mainly used for wine tastings, luncheons and dinners. More intimate events take place in a 17th-century townhouse on Pickering Place, a secret Georgian cul-de-sac adjacent to the shop, site of the country's last duel. A four-hour luncheon in the Long Room, an elegant vision of damask

wallpaper and polished mahogany, is surely one of the most decadent ways to spend a Monday afternoon.

Contrary to expectation, a leisurely lunch designed as an introduction to Spanish wines was not remotely intimidating – and there's not a Rioja in sight. Our hosts, Lance Jefferson and Francis Huicq, are passionate, eloquent and witty. They take questions with genuine interest. Remarkably, they're just as articulate after sampling seven wines – though they wisely refrain from draining their glasses, unlike the rest of us.

We started with crisp Gramona cava, which brought a whiff of Mediterranean summer to drizzly London. Two contrasting whites from the coastal region of Galicia set off basil-crusted sardines with *piquillo* pepper salsa and Gordal olives stuffed with chorizo. The wines were exceptional but the food is no afterthought: chef Stewart Turner is a protégé of Michel Roux Jr. Slow-roast pork belly with *pata negra* and apple purée packed a punch, rather like the 2007 Pesquera Reserva. ("Nothing like those Spanish head-bangers we used to know," as Lance noted drily.) We savoured a 1996 Torresilo from Ribero del Duero slowly with a trio of Spanish cheeses, served with *pan de higo*, *membrillo* and oat biscuits. An ethereal macadamia nut parfait with prune spring rolls and Earl Grey jelly almost outshone a smooth, amber East India Solera sherry. In centuries past, casks of sherry were lashed to ships sailing for the Indies as ballast. With all that extra ballast, thankfully we weren't subjected to a weigh-in on the shop scales on our way out.

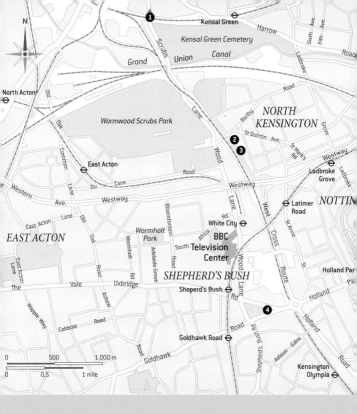

WEST LONDON

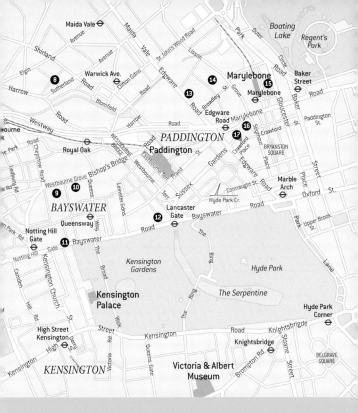

CENTRO GALEGO DE LONDRES

869 Harrow Road, Willesden, NW10 5NG
- 020 8964 4873
- www.centrogalegodelondres.com
- Open Mon–Thurs noon–10pm; Fri, Sat noon–11.30pm; Sun noon–9.30pm
- Transport Willesden Junction rail or tube
- Budget

> **Top-class tapas at knockdown prices**

Stretching from Edgware Road to Willesden, Harrow Road is one of those dreary expanses of no man's land that Londoners drive through in a hurry. But there are a few nuggets of culinary brilliance lodged between the pound shops and fried chicken joints. On a particularly desolate strip, where Harrow Road tails off into Harlesden, this cosy social club is where Galician expats gather to gossip over giant portions of authentic Spanish food.

It doesn't look like much from the outside. But pull up a stool at the tapas bar and there's an unmistakable air of Mediterranean bonhomie, from the generous glug of Rias Baixas to the bulging basket of bread and butter. Through the kitchen hatch, you can watch the chefs slicing fluffy mounds of boiled potatoes to turn into a moist, melting tortilla – a treat that's often thrown in free with your first glass of wine.

At the handful of tables, stocky Spaniards tuck into enormous plates of paella and steaks the size of skis. I prefer to sample as many dishes as possible from the selection of fantastic and fantastically cheap tapas. Despite several visits with equally voracious friends, I haven't managed to try everything. However, I can wholeheartedly recommend the *pulpo con cachelos* (boiled octopus and potatoes dusted with rock salt and smoked paprika), *pimientos de padron* (flash-fried baby peppers that will occasionally blow your head off), and *chorizo al vino* (punchy garlic sausage cooked in Rioja). Seafood is a Galician speciality and my prawn-loving pals go crazy for the *gambas al ajillo* (garlicky tails of king prawn).

Downstairs are two larger dining rooms that appear to be trapped in Spanish suburbia circa 1980 (napkin fans, random folk art, trophies from the resident football club, Deportivo Galicia, founded in 1968 like the Centro Galego itself). On Friday and Saturday nights, diners are entertained with (deafening) live music. One evening in August, I stumbled upon a traditional festival, with revellers in horned helmets playing the bagpipes. Apparently, this raucous ritual commemorates Galicia's Celtic roots.

The best time to visit is during a football match featuring any Spanish team. Crowded into every corner are extended families in football strips, men chewing over tactics between mouthfuls of monkfish stew, anxious fans knocking back Estrella beers. The whole place erupts whenever the Spaniards score and if the right team wins you'll be hugging and dancing with strangers. I can't wait for the next World Cup.

TUNG TONG

308 Latimer Road, North Kensington, W10 6QU
- 020 8960 5988
- www.tungtong.co.uk
- Open Mon–Fri noon–3pm, 6–11pm; Sat 6–11pm, Sun 6–10.30pm
- Transport Latimer Road or White City tube
- Budget

Oodles of noodles

Like the rival Thai restaurant a few blocks away (*see below*), Tung Tong seems to have an identity crisis. Formerly known as Thai River, it's been renamed after a famous Thai dish – crispy wonton parcels of minced meat, shredded vegetables and crushed peanuts – that isn't even on the menu. Tung Tong literally means "money bags", but this diminutive canteen is cheap as can be.

Semi-industrial and down at heel, Latimer Road isn't pretty, but Tung Tong sure is. The corner building is swathed in so much ivy that the restaurant sign is barely visible. A miniature picket fence leads into a secret "tropical garden" draped in vines and fairy lights, with Buddha statuettes peeping out between the foliage. A few tables are squeezed in here, with several more in the simple, softly lit interior.

In a residential area with limited transport links, the clientele consists entirely of loyal locals. The menu covers all the Thai classics – fish cakes, prawn toasts, sweet and sour soups, sizzling stir-fries, assorted red, green and jungle curries. There are more unusual items too, such as *kao soi* (egg noodles in coconut curry topped with more deep-fried noodles, a dish from northern Thailand) and the alarmingly named Pinky in Blanket (marinated prawns wrapped in deep-fried rice paper). While not quite as fiery or zingy as the finest Thai restaurants, every dish tastes and looks homemade.

There's a charming amateurishness about the whole affair, from the random radio soundtrack to the unfailingly friendly young staff, who speak almost no English (which can be problematic for allergy sufferers like me). You almost feel as if you're eating in someone's living room. This sense of cosy familiarity is confirmed by the restaurant's mission statement: "We have no goal in business just make our customers happy with everything is our intention."

NEARBY

FITOU

(1 Dalgarno Gardens, North Kensington, W10 6AB; 020 8968 0558, www.fitourestaurant.co.uk)

Despite a cult following among locals, very few outsiders know about this chilli-lovers' paradise tucked away beside Little Wormwood Scrubs park. Previously the No 1 Thai Café, what was a hole-in-the-wall has expanded into a fully-fledged restaurant. Skip the Malaysian dishes and stick with the eye-watering Thai menu. When they say hot, they mean HOT. Safer bets for wimpier palates are crispy duck pancakes in hoisin sauce and a perfect pad Thai.

ARIADNE'S NEKTAR

274 Latimer Road, North Kensington, W10 6QU
- 020 8968 8212
- Open noon–midnight daily, but call ahead to check
- Transport White City or Latimer Road tube
- Moderate

> *Master and margarita (plus moussaka)*

The first clue that this isn't your typical boozer is the Greek flag flying outside. Then there are the two motorbikes parked inside, and the photograph of the naked landlord astride one of them hanging by the toilets. Ariadne's Nektar is the kind of place where someone might stroll up to the bar in a gorilla suit (which happened to me one night). It's a seemingly low-key bar where you strike up conversations with strangers, accidentally get slaughtered on a Monday night, and end up necking your neighbour (which happened to a friend of mine).

The maverick behind this work of genius is Dimitri, the most irascible landlord in London. A former lawyer who enjoys modelling his collection of wigs and hats, Dimitri likes nothing better than a fierce debate (as long as he wins the argument). Just don't get him started on Greek etymology or the politics of civil disobedience. If he's in a good mood, Dimitri will break out his stash of *tsipouro* (Cretan grappa) and home-cured olives. If you inadvertently rile him, he will treat you to "a bollocking free of charge". Anyone who has spent time in Greece will appreciate that this particular form of abuse is usually reserved for favoured patrons.

Named after Dimitri's beautiful daughter, Ariadne's Nektar is a local in the real sense of the word. With its ragged collection of antiques and cosy lighting, it's like straying into someone's living room. The usual suspects propping up the bar are bohemian local residents, pretty things from the textile design studio next door, and musicians stumbling in after a session at The Grove recording studios across the road. Occasionally, bands stage live shows or impromptu jam sessions in the pub. Otherwise, patrons are well served by Dimitri's sweeping music collection, which ranges from Gorillaz to Dizzy Gillespie.

The legendary Thursday night pub quiz is sadly no more, but in summer you can quaff margaritas and mojitos, made with generous Mediterranean-style measures, at the handful of tables outside. After too many cocktails, fortify yourself with Dimitri's delicious spanakopitta and moussaka – although he only cooks when the mood takes him. Dimitri keeps threatening to sell up and retire to a Greek island, so go and experience his unconventional hospitality while you can. But be warned: the opening hours are as unpredictable as the owner.

GINGLIK

❹

1 Shepherd's Bush Green, Shepherd's Bush, W12 8PH
• 020 7348 8968 • www.ginglik.co.uk
• Open Mon–Thurs 7pm–closing time varies, Fri, Sat 7pm–3am (sometimes 4am), Sun 7pm–12.30am; open from 9pm Fri, Sat in June, July and August
• Transport Shepherd's Bush tube
• Moderate

Spend a penny

The East End may have got all the attention (and some pretty dubious "regeneration") in the run-up to the 2012 Olympics, but London's first Olympics were held at the opposite end of town in Shepherd's Bush. The 1908 Games were supposed to be staged in Rome, but when Vesuvius erupted in 1906 the Italian authorities pulled out and London stepped in. A stadium was hastily erected in ten months, named "White City" after its whitewashed steel and concrete structure. The stadium was demolished in the 1980s to make way for a BBC Media Centre, but the public toilets built to service the spectators streaming out of Shepherd's Bush underground station have survived.

Between times a subterranean snooker hall, in 2002 Tammi Willis and Colin Welsh converted the Edwardian loos into "an independent beat bunker" that hosts live music, comedy, cabaret and club nights. In the middle of a traffic-clogged junction, the inconspicuous entrance is next to the war memorial on Shepherd's Bush Green. (Look for the fairy lights wrapped around the railings.) Downstairs, it's dark, a little damp, and slightly dingy, but the energy is warm and positive (although the loos are pretty shabby for a venue that started life as a public convenience). The club is members only, but a free pay-as-you-go membership on the door gets you and four guests entry, subject to any admission charges.

Ginglik is a Cantonese martial arts term meaning "explosive power". Every Monday night, the space is used for Wing Chun classes for wannabe Bruce Lees (which explains the armless wooden dummy in the bar). Otherwise, the line-up covers all bases – Balkan DJs, a Japanese *theremin* orchestra, the best of London's buskers. Paloma Faith, Paolo Nutini and Ellie Goulding all performed at The Big Secret, a weekly showcase for emerging singer/songwriters, before they became famous. The fortnightly comedy nights have also introduced some big names to the scene. Robin Williams even put in a surprise appearance before performing at The Royal Variety Show.

On a recent comedy night, the MC took one look at the crowd and snorted: "You're the most white, middle class audience I've ever seen." That was nothing compared to the next act, the brilliantly offbeat Lou Sanders: my friend was laughing so hard, Sanders accused her of being on poppers.

NEARBY

FM
(Hopgood Street, W12 7JU; 020 8811 2807; www.fm184.com)
This Philillippino karaoke club gets wild at weekends, when it stays open until 3am.

SPORTING CLUBE DE LONDRES 5

27 Elkstone Road, Notting Hill, W10 5NP
- 020 8968 3069
- www.sportingclubedelondres.com
- Open Tues–Thurs 1–11pm, Fri 1pm–1.30am, Sat 1pm–2am, Sun 1pm–midnight; closed Mon
- Transport Westbourne Park tube
- Moderate

A secret club for soccer fans

At the tail end of Portobello market, Golborne Road is a scruffy jumble of junk shops, Moroccan delis, and Portuguese bakeries that has miraculously escaped gentrification – at least for now. As well as some of the best tagines in London, you'll find the finest *pasteis de nata* (custard tarts) at Lisboa Patisserie, a spartan café permanently abustle with sweet-toothed Portuguese.

But the real hub of the local Portuguese community is a few blocks away, lodged between a skate park and a council estate on Elkstone Road. A green banner emblazoned with "SCL" is the only clue that this extraordinary restaurant isn't a derelict warehouse. Sporting Clube de Londres opened in 1991 as a social club for the eponymous football team of Portuguese expats.

Portugal is a nation of football fanatics. So it's no surprise the walls are lined with football shirts and trophies, and soccer games are shown on giant screens. When there's no match on, Portuguese soaps are played on a loop.

Mid-week the cavernous dining room – all gold chairs and slot machines – is sparsely populated with regulars, who are treated like family by the soft-spoken owner, Rui Daniel Faria Velosa, and his formidable wife. Like any authentic Portuguese restaurant, portions are gigantic and vegetables are an afterthought. Salt cod croquettes, octopus with paprika, and spicy chorizo are followed by platters of *peri peri* chicken, steaming pans of seafood paella, and dangling skewers of succulent meat, the fat dripping onto a heap of home-made chips. It's highly unlikely you'll have the space (or inclination) to sample the fluorescent cakes on display in an illuminated fridge. Molotoff, a cross between meringue pie and crème caramel, is bound to have an explosive effect on your digestive system.

On sunny weekends, there are alfresco barbeques in the yard and bingo sessions every Sunday afternoon. Visit on Friday or Saturday night and the mood is markedly different. The football fans are substituted by boisterous parties of friends and relatives who come for the live music. The entertainment consists of a paunchy crooner performing karaoke versions of Donna Summer, The Gypsy Kings, Elvis and The Police in a heavy Portuguese accent. The skinny-hipped head-waiter, Bruno, snakes between the tables, mincing to the music and calling everyone "darling". Medallion men down shots of *aguardente* at the bar, while toddlers and teenagers burn up the dance floor until well past midnight.

BOOKS FOR COOKS

4 Blenheim Crescent, Notting Hill, W11 1NN
- 020 7221 1992
- www.booksforcooks.com
- Open Tues–Sat 10am–6pm (cake and coffee: 10am–noon, lunch: noon–2pm) Closed last three weeks in August and 10 days over Christmas.
- Transport Ladbroke Grove or Notting Hill Gate tube
- Budget

Try before you buy

Cooking the books isn't always to be frowned upon. The aromas wafting from the kitchen at the back of this culinary bookshop are even more tempting than the appetite-whetting wares that line the shelves. Hungry customers put a selection of recipes from these cookbooks to the test every day.

This Notting Hill institution has become a sort of secret society for foodies. Nurse Heidi Lascelles set up Books for Cooks in 1983. "At that time, British cooking was a standing joke the world over," the shop's website admits. Former resident cooks Annie Bell and Clarissa Dickson Wright soon changed that.

Today, in the open kitchen, a trio of indefatigable chefs – Eric, Clara, and Marylou – produce some of the best value lunches in London. The two- or three-course set menu is always different. Dishes of the day (tweeted to their followers every morning) depend on what's in season. Ingredients are sourced locally from Portobello market, the Moroccan and Portuguese delis on Golborne Road, and The Spice Shop across the street. Organic meat comes from Sheepdrove farm. Lunch might feature lentil and saffron soup, stuffed pork with sage polenta, and upside down pear and ginger pudding. Sweet-toothed locals come for a daily fix of freshly baked cake. Orange meringue, chocolate and Guinness, double ginger, cinnamon swirl with sour cream - all have legions of devotees.

A few stray tourists venture in on Fridays and Saturdays, when Portobello market is in full swing. "Some people come in expecting us to be the bookshop from *Notting Hill*," sighs manager Rosie Hogg. The story of the current owners could be mistaken for a cheesy Hollywood script. In 1992, Rosie Kindersley walked into the shop as a customer and walked out an employee. When chef Eric Treuillé sauntered into Books for Cooks a year later, it was coup de foudre. The couple took over the business in 2001.

There are compilations of the test kitchen's greatest hits on the till, so you can try to recreate your lunch at home. Demonstrations and tastings are held upstairs, accompanied with wine from Eric's biodynamic vineyard in France. Occasional supper clubs were introduced in summer 2011.

With only a handful of tables, the only drawback is that the food runs out fast - so go early. The cramped, colourful eating area isn't a place to linger; but that's a small price to pay for food that's so affordable and exciting. I'm sure their accounts are above reproach, too.

UNDER THE WESTWAY

242 Acklam Road, Westbourne Park, W10 5JJ
- 020 7575 3123
- www.utww.co.uk
- Open Mon–Thurs 9am–9pm, Fri, Sat 9am–2.30am
Restaurant open for dinner 8–11pm, reservation only
Club nights are members only. To join, email guestlist@utww.co.uk or call
020 7575 3123
- Transport Westbourne Park or Ladbroke Grove tube
- Moderate

> **Head out on the highway, looking for adventure**

It may have featured in songs by The Clash (*London's Burning*) and Blur (*For Tomorrow*), but the Westway is surely one of London's most unattractive road. When it opened in 1970, this elevated dual carriageway linking Paddington and North Kensington was the largest continuous concrete structure in Britain.

Today, much of the derelict land cleared to make way for the Westway has been turned into sports centres and skate parks. But one section of highway is the roof of a secret café and club. Under the Westway is inside Westbourne Studios, a giant bunker that's home to about 100 creative businesses, from record labels to graphic designers. The huge atrium is dotted with potted palms and pool tables, and surrounded by glass-walled studios filled with people whose jobs look more interesting than yours. At the back is a bar with leatherette booths and sofas. The ceiling is the underbelly of the motorway – it's not even insulated, just sloping slabs of raw concrete. But you can't hear the thunder of traffic overhead above the hum of hipness.

By day, it's a staff canteen, serving predictable but keenly priced burgers, salads, spag bol and the like. (The Westway burger topped with haloumi, bacon and mayo is good). Fancier fare is served in the evenings. At weekends, "eatings and meetings" give way to after-hours dancing. It feels like a house party – casual, unpretentious and friendly. "It's what a pub would be like if they didn't kick everyone out at 11pm," says Etienne Vicard, one half of the Gallo-Greek management team. "It's a place where things happen." There's a giant projector for screenings and the sound system is top-notch – hardly surprising with all the musicians in the house. The most famous resident, Blur's Damon Albarn, has moved on. But there's still a chance you'll meet the next big thing at the bar.

TSIAKKOS & CHARCOAL

8

5 Marylands Road, Maida Vale, W9 2DU
• 020 7286 7896
• Open Tues–Sat 7–11pm
• Transport Royal Oak, Warwick Avenue or Maida Vale tube,
then 10–15 minute walk; bus 18
• Budget (cash only)

As Greek as it gets

I'd often walked past this neighbourhood restaurant and assumed it was closed. A pirate flag and some drab curtains are drawn across the windows, the door is always shut, and the lights seem to be permanently off. Nudge open the door, squeeze past empty beer crates, unpaid bills, a man playing the spoons, and a pair of teenage boys stalking girls on Facebook, and you have arrived at London's finest Cypriot restaurant.

The food is sensational and the mood is Mediterranean holiday. Xenis Pitsiali, in beard and baseball cap, mans the barbeque, grilling kebabs and bantering with friends and family members without breaking sweat. He's been doing this five nights a week for 15 years, but it's obvious he's still enjoying himself. Xen's parents arrived in London as political refugees from Cyprus in the early 60s and opened a café on Portobello Road. When the owner of his family's favourite Greek restaurant retired, Xen took over. His three sons George, Grigoris and Alberto ("named after my wife's dad, my dad, and Alberto Ascari, a racing driver") take turns waiting tables. It's very much a family business –and Xen's regulars are part of the family.

Guests squeeze into the cosy, wood-panelled dining room or the secret garden, clad in bamboo and strung with multicoloured lights. There are candles in beer bottles, a headless statue, and battered sofas for smokers. The computer playlist, often hijacked by customers, veers between Barry White, Pulp and David Bowie.

There's no wine list, just cheap house plonk or KEO beer. The menu, scrawled on a ripped sheet of paper, never changes. It covers all the Cypriot classics: tarama, humus, haloumi, aromatic basturma sausages, beetroot spiked with garlic, stewed beans, and Greek salad with a giant chunk of feta. Xen will tell you when he thinks his tarama isn't up to par. If it scores ten out of ten, Xen tapes a cross on the window. Apart from grilled sea bream, mains are meaty. You must order *kleftiko*, a hunk of juicy, crisp-skinned lamb dripping into a heap of clove and cinnamon pilaf, or Xen's signature dish of "slow-burnt pork", marinated in ginger, garlic and lemon squash. "It used to be called slow-cooked pork, but I changed the name after I burnt the Christmas dinner for the team at Books for Cooks" (see p. 83).

As the name suggests, you'll leave smelling of charcoal – the lingering aroma of that delicious burnt pork and another bright night at Xen's.

NEARBY

WATERSIDE CAFÉ
(Warwick Crescent, Little Venice, W2 6NE; 020 7266 4665)
On a barge moored in Little Venice, this canal-side café is a great escape from
all things urban. Service can be curt, but the setting is idyllic.

INAHO

4 Hereford Road, Bayswater, W2 4AA
- 020 7221 8495
- Open Mon–Fri 12.30–2.30pm, Mon–Sat 7–11pm, closed Sun
- Transport Royal Oak or Bayswater tube
- Moderate

Box clever

Restaurants come and go on Westbourne Grove and its offshoot, Hereford Road. But not Inaho. Celebrating its twentieth anniversary in 2011, this diminutive Japanese eaterie looks like a shack from the outside. But take a closer look behind the indigo drapes and hanging plants and you'll see a lucky cat waving in the window. The boxy, wood-panelled dining room is like wandering into someone's living room in the back streets of Tokyo.

Chunky wooden tables squeezed close together create a cosy atmosphere (in which you can't help eavesdropping on your neighbours). The irresistible sizzle of tempura drifts through from the kitchen, screened behind a curtain. The same chef, S. Otsuka, has been turning out home-style Japanese dishes since the day Inaho opened in April 1991.

With a staff of just four, including owner N. Nakamura, service is inevitably haphazard. On arrival, the waitress brings you a dainty dish of crispy salmon skin or mackerel in *ponzu* sauce to whet your appetite while you wait. I always order the sticky aubergine with sweet *miso* sauce and homemade pickles (*konomono*) right away – the perfect complement to chilled *reishu* sake.

Be sure to ask for the specials menu of small sharing dishes (*osusume-hin* – literally, "what do you recommend?") This *izakaya*-style fare might include standout dishes like *hijiki nimono* (braised black seaweed), *ika geso age* (grilled squid tentacles), *hamachi kama shioyaki* (salt-grilled yellowtail collar), and *toro kakuni* (slow-stewed tuna belly). The succession of dishes arrives in random order, whenever they're ready. Everything is artfully presented on traditional crockery that's so pretty you'll want to steal it. Steaming "sumo hot pots" are miracle cures for hangovers and set lunches in lacquered bento boxes are enormously comforting. For dessert, the sesame seed and green tea ice cream is as subtle and surprising as everything else on the menu.

Intimate and unstuffy, Inaho is a great date venue. There are only ten tables, so you must book. Oddly, I've rarely seen Japanese people eating here, but Americans seem to love it. Prices are a little steep, but I never resent paying over the odds for food this good served in such delicious surroundings.

THE TIROLER HUT

27 Westbourne Grove, Bayswater, W2 4UA
- 020 7727 3981
- www.tirolerhut.co.uk
- Open Tues–Sat 6.30pm–1am, Sun 6.30–11pm
- Transport Bayswater, Royal Oak or Queensway tube
- Moderate

Austrian sing-alongs

The website promises "a lively evening of entertainment including Yodelling, Accordion and the highly original Tyrolean Cow Bell Cabaret". Lively is an understatement. Nothing could prepare you for the nightly performance at this temple to Austrian kitsch.

First, you have to get past the chain-smoking, 70-something doorman, who relishes keeping the weekend crowds at bay. Midweek, you'll have no problem squeezing into the mock-Alpine basement bunker, all gingham curtains, wooden beams, and 1970s' posters of blondes on ski slopes. Barmaids in heaving dirndls ply the regulars at the bar with shots of schnapps, while paunchy waiters in lederhosen lubricate the diners with flagons of lager. Josep, a stocky little waiter, can carry six steins in each hand. "I am Leo and dragon, unfortunately not octopus," Josep quips, as he tries to clear the plates of one especially blotto party. This place must be keeping Jagermeister afloat.

A poster of a chimp eating pancakes and drinking a pint sets the mood for the food. The menu – a pork and stodge fest – hasn't changed since Tiroler Hut opened in 1967: there's liver dumpling soup, bratwurst with sauerkraut, schnitzel, or the heart-stopping "*Mir ist alles Wurst*" (mixed fried sausage ensemble). I've never dared to try any of it, but the ladies all seem to favour fondue.

You don't come here for the food; you come for the entertainment. The live music usually starts around 8.30pm. Barricaded in a wooden booth plastered with alpine paraphernalia, a one-man orchestra on a glockenspiel and accordion pounds out a medley that lurches between Elvis, Dolly Parton, Santana and Zorba the Greek. "I'd rather play only Austrian songs, but later on people want a bit of razzmatazz," says Joseph Friedmann, the Hungarian owner and star attraction, whose Austrian wife Christina inspired the Tyrolean theme. His grand finale is a rendition of *Edelweiss* played on a set of cow bells. The whole room sings along, noisily and tunelessly. Friedmann is in his element, although he's been performing the same routine every night for over 40 years. "Not every night," he grins. "We're closed on Mondays."

Surprisingly for somewhere so deeply unfashionable, the Tiroler Hut is a hit with the fashion crowd. A collage of photos commemorates the celebrities who've enjoyed a spot of yodelling, including Claudia Schiffer, Vivienne Westwood, and a naked Juergen Teller face down in a platter of suckling pig. "The internet has helped us a lot," says Friedmann. "Especially as we have Kate Moss on our website – people think she's here every night."

CAFÉ DIANA

5 Wellington Terrace, Bayswater Road, Notting Hill, W2 4LW
- 020 7792 9606;
- Open 8am–11pm daily
- Transport Notting Hill tube
- Moderate (cash only)

To Di for

"**S**he always sat at the same table – right where you were sitting."
I'm convinced that Fouad Fatah uses the same line on all his customers. Unlike me, most of them are massive fans of this café's namesake and erstwhile neighbour, Princess Diana. The paparazzi who lay in wait for the princess to emerge from Kensington Palace would sustain themselves with tea and toast at this modest little caff, opposite the ostentatious embassies and oligarchs' mansions lined up along Kensington Palace Gardens. Diana herself even dropped in occasionally.

Fatah's boss, Abdul Doaud, opened the café in 1989. "We came up with the name and five days later Princess Diana was in for a coffee. She brought the first signed picture of herself, and we just carried on." Now the walls are plastered in portraits of "the people's princess": Diana in a splendid succession of 80s' outfits, a montage of her changing hairstyles, Diana jogging, white water rafting, smiling coyly, a signed photograph with the café staff. There are three framed thank-you letters expressing Diana's appreciation for the birthday bouquets sent to her by Abdul. Diana's private secretary, Patrick Jephson, clearly had a florid way with words: "*Though they mark the inexorable passage of another year, they are no less appreciated.*" The final letter, a personal note from Diana – "*I am deeply touched that you have thought of me in this special way*"– is dated July 1, 1997, the month before her death.

Diana often brought princes William and Harry here for an English breakfast. "She was too normal – a regular mum. She said hello to everyone, always coming down to our level," Fatah gushes. "And she always insisted on paying." The café charges royally for distinctly plebeian fare –scrambled eggs, shish kebabs, toasted sandwiches, and chips with everything. I doubt the Princess ever indulged in "Diana's dishes" such as deep-fried chicken escalope. "She looked after her figure, but she loved her cappuccinos and sometimes even had a croissant," Fatah confides.

Diana fanatics from all over the world come here to pay their respects. "Too many, it never stops! I don't think so they will ever forget her." Apparently, Prince Harry recently pressed his face to the window, gazing wistfully at all the photographs. Now that Prince William has moved into his mother's old digs at Kensington Palace, perhaps he and Kate will become regulars? "Oh yes, we expect him to pop in soon."

BEL CANTO

1 Lancaster Gate, Bayswater, W2 3LG
- 020 7262 1678
- www.lebelcanto.com
- Open Tues–Sat 7–11pm
- Transport Lancaster Gate or Paddington tube
- Moderate

**_Singing
with your supper_**

If you love to hate AA Gill, the scathing restaurant critic of *The Sunday Times*, you might enjoy Bel Canto. Gill's review of this operatic eaterie's former incarnation in the City was so excoriating that it closed within months. Having tasted success with two similar ventures in Paris, owner Jean-Paul Maurel did not despair. Instead, he moved to a basement below the distinctly unglamorous Corus Hotel Hyde Park. "The hotel owner is my number one fan", Maurel confides.

Pick your way through the glum patrons drinking lukewarm beer and watching football in the lobby. Downstairs, the decor is just on the safe side

of kitsch: burgundy walls, soft lighting, headless mannequins in low-cut costumes. An expectant hush hovers over the dolled-up couples picking over a set menu of uninspired but respectably executed French standards. Like the waiting staff, wines are divided into mezzos, baritones, sopranos and tenors.

Between courses, the servers burst into arias from Puccini and Verdi. There's a song every 15 minutes, which inevitably makes for some stilted conversations. It might be excruciating, except the singers are really rather good. Most of them alternate occasional nights here with performances on much grander stages. Weaving between the tables, graciously fielding musical or culinary questions as they hand over your beef fillet or apple tart, they seem to relish the opportunity to try out lead roles or rehearse for auditions before a live audience. Each night is different, with the diners' reactions as varied as the repertoire. A concert pianist tinkles away throughout.

The crescendo comes with dessert. Singers toast each table with prosecco while belting out Brindisi from *La Traviata*. Their performance is so heartfelt that even staid Middle Englanders and bashful Japanese couples are persuaded to sing along with gusto.

Aimed at those who think opera is elitist or over-priced, Bel Canto makes for a slightly surreal, high camp but thoroughly entertaining evening. Just don't take any of it too seriously. And come early – doors open at 7pm and the grand finale is around 9.30pm.

MANDALAY

444 Edgware Road, W2 1EG;
- 020 7258 3696
- www.mandalayway.com
- Open Mon—Sat noon—2.30pm, 6—10.30pm
- Transport Edgware Road tube
- Budget

*Authentic
Asian fusion*

Buried between the Middle Eastern shisha bars of Marble Arch and the fancy eateries of Maida Vale, Mandalay bills itself as London's only Burmese restaurant. In fact, it's more like a Rangoon greasy spoon, with gaudy plastic tablecloths, faded posters of Buddhist temples, and a bouquet of fake roses on the kitchen counter. But as soon as you open the laminated menu, you'll know you've hit upon something special.

A fusion of Thai, Chinese and Indian culinary influences, Burmese food is less spicy, greasy and rich than those cuisines. Flavoured with coconut milk, tamarind, lemongrass or fish sauce, most dishes aren't especially spicy (ask for chillies on the side if you want to ramp up the heat). A shredded papaya and cucumber salad makes a zingy foil for crunchy fritters of leafy greens or shrimp and bean sprouts, served with mango, soy and tamarind dipping sauces. Of the seafood dishes, the best is *bazun-kya khauk-swe* – noodles with king prawns in a rich coconut and turmeric sauce (like a milder version of Malaysian *laksa*). Another Burmese classic not to be missed is *mokhingar* ("snack soup"), rice vermicelli in fish broth, traditionally eaten for breakfast. The Burmese word for vegetarian literally means "avoid killing life", so there's an unusual selection of vegetables too.

All these dishes – and many more soups, samosas, curries and stir-fries – are produced in a cramped kitchen screened off from the dining room. Portions are pretty small, but prices are low and lunch deals are great value. The wine list is basic (stick to Tiger beer) and desserts are not for the fainthearted: frighteningly blue agar-agar jelly or shocking-pink faluda, a South-East Asian knickerbocker glory made of ice cream, tapioca, jelly and rose syrup.

Mandalay was opened in 1994 by Burmese brothers Dwight Altaf and Gary Iqbal Ally, whose wives take it in turns to do the cooking. The Ally brothers have an illustrious heritage: their great-uncle, Dr Ba Maw, was the first Prime Minister of Burma when it became a British colony in 1937, and their great-aunt was the first Burmese woman to serve in the United Nations. But this grandeur is nowhere in evidence in the grubby toilets out in the back yard – a less than appetising experience.

Most savoury dishes are covered in fried onions and garlic, so it's probably not the best venue for a date. But for a casual, cosy and cheap nosh-up with friends, family or intrepid out-of-towners, Mandalay is a safe bet – as long as you book ahead for dinner, as there's only space for 28.

ALFIES ROOFTOP RESTAURANT

Alfies Antique Market, 13–25 Church Street, Marylebone, NW8 8DT
• 020 7706 2969
• www.alfiesantiques.com/cafe.php
• Open Tues–Sat 10am–6pm
• Transport Marylebone or Edgware Road tube
• Budget (cash & cheque only)

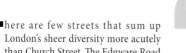

*Fryer
on the roof*

There are few streets that sum up London's sheer diversity more acutely than Church Street. The Edgware Road end is a blur of cheap fruit and falafel stalls, which give way to elegant antique shops as you approach Lisson Grove. Burqa-clad ladies rummage through heaps of sequined fabrics and gleaming aubergines, while vintage aficionados get their flat white fix from the Indie Coffee cart – the only sign of encroaching gentrification in this unfashionable street market.

In the midst of this frenetic hawking and haggling is Alfies, an Art Deco department store converted into an antiques emporium back in 1976. It was founded by Bennie Gray, who also set up Gray's antiques market in a 19th-century toilet factory in Mayfair. Alfie was the name of his father, "a brilliant jazz musician, but sadly, not a great antique dealer". The pistachio and lemon façade of Alfies looks good enough to eat, but the polished wares inside are even more tempting – provided you have very deep pockets.

If the antiques are out of your league, you can find a bargain at the secret rooftop café. Despite a spruce up in summer 2011 (punters were asked to vote for their preferred colour of paint), there's nothing fancy about this place, with its plastic chairs and sizzling deep fryer. Sadly, the Wurlitzer jukebox is for display only. The menu is limited to full English breakfasts, baked potatoes, burgers and sandwiches. The food may be unimaginative, but huge portions are well priced and served with a smile by manager Mark and his friendly team.

But the real draw is the large, hidden terrace, with views across the rooftops to the BT Tower to the east and the glossy office blocks of Paddington Basin to the west. Standing guard before a mural of an ancient Greek temple, a pair of caryatids stare out across the skyline. On sunny afternoons, local residents come here with the newspapers to catch some rays. Wheeler-dealers wind each other up over bacon sandwiches and interior designers take a break from maxing out their clients' credit cards downstairs. Couples have even got hitched up here, the bridesmaids in period dresses and quiffs courtesy of Nina's, a beauty parlour on the first floor that specialises in retro makeovers.

Kingsley Amis **JAKE'S THING**

DICKENS — A TALE OF TWO CITIES

THOMAS HARDY Tess of the D'Urbervilles   **WILBUR SMITH**

WILBUR SMITH THE ANGELS WEEP

FRANKENSTEIN Mary Shelley   TEACH YOUR SON OR DAUGHTER TO DRIVE   Thomas Walsh The Eye of...

le Carré   **THE TAILOR OF PANAMA**

NO COMEBACKS

SWAN & EDGAR

43 Linhope Street, Marylebone, NW1 6HL
- 020 7724 6268
- www.swanandedgar.co.uk
- Open Mon–Sat 4–11pm, Sun noon–10.30pm
- Transport Marylebone tube or rail
- Moderate

*A local
with a novel
approach*

Bourne and Hollingsworth started out as an underground speakeasy, a sneaky hideout among the flashy cocktail bars of Charlotte Street. Hot on the vintage heels of its sell-out Blitz and Prohibition parties, B&H has become a victim of its own popularity. But its sister venue, the Swan & Edgar (named after another defunct London department store), happily remains just under the radar.

Situated on a perfect little backstreet behind Marylebone station, this tiny boozer has been around since at least the 1930s. Formerly known as The Feathers, it's a classic local pub – a rarity in London these days, as corporate chains and property developers take over more and more premises. But the Swan & Edgar's interior is not your typical combo of nicotine-stained walls and sticky carpets. The bookshelf above the doorway is a giveaway: the decor is inspired by all things legible and alphabetical. The idea came from the practice of concealing menus in paperbacks at Bourne and Hollingsworth.

It took thirty consecutive hours to build the bar out of stacks of paperbacks donated by friends. Chairs, shelves and cornices are covered in old copies of The Financial Times. The bathroom floors are made of Scrabble tiles. (You could spend ages locked in the loo, looking for a "Swan", an "Edgar" and a "Bourne". There's even a Russian letter hidden there, in honour of the Russian co-owner, Anya). The banquettes aren't bookish, but are lined with recycled off-cuts from Savile Row tailors.

Don't bother with the indifferent food – stick to the small but affordable wine list. With space for only a handful of tables, there's a cosy, informal atmosphere compounded by the laissez-faire attitude of the staff. It's easy to strike up conversations with strangers, as you can't really help eavesdropping on them. Upstairs is an even more intimate room that's perfect for whispering sweet couplets into your date's ear. Smokers battle for the benches outside, where you can puff away and fantasise about moving into one of the gorgeous Georgian townhouses opposite – a hop and a skip away from Regent's Park and the ultimate local pub. Dream on.

DININGS

22 Harcourt Street, Marylebone, W1H 4HH
- 020 7723 0666
- www.dinings.co.uk
- Open Mon–Fri noon–2.30pm and 6–10.30pm, Sat 6–10.30pm
- Transport Edgware Road tube or Marylebone rail
- Expensive

As small as a cat's forehead

This "Japanese tapas" restaurant is a closely guarded secret among London foodies, mainly because it's so small that it can only hold about two dozen diners. In Japan, they'd call it *neko no hitai* ("as small as a cat's forehead").

Opening a minuscule restaurant on a residential backstreet in Marylebone might not seem like a smart business move, especially when the dining room is a windowless basement designed like a bunker. The toilets are so minute that you have to manoeuvre your way through one door before you can open the other. The six-seat sushi counter upstairs is right by the front door, and every time a diner arrives the chefs yell out "*Irashaimase*" ("Welcome to my house" in Japanese). This annoying habit of shouting at every guest is a hangover from head chef Masaki Sugisaki's days at Nobu.

Despite these drawbacks, Dinings has a cult following and I'm one of its devotees. Sugisaki's experimental menu is not for purists. Traditional Japanese flavours (*ponzu, miso, yuzu*) are paired with unorthodox ingredients such as coriander, truffle and foie gras with (mostly) brilliant results. Young European waiters, who almost outnumber the customers, glide up and down the stairs between kitchen and dining room bearing a succession of exquisitely plated delicacies. Sea bass carpaccio with shavings of black truffle, minced onion, and cubes of *ponzu* jelly hit you with intense bursts of flavour. Seared *wagyu* beef drizzled in *ponzu* and porcini oil is meaty, earthy and musky. Grilled chilli and garlic black cod is unctuous, without the cloying sweetness usually associated with this fish. Ethereal tempura comes with three dipping sauces that tease out different flavours. Refreshing raspberry and mandarin sorbet and *hoji* tea round things off nicely.

All this culinary craftsmanship comes at a high price, although the *osusume* set lunch selections of *sushi, nigiri* and *donburi* are excellent value for food this good.

NEARBY

GEORGE BAR

(Durrants Hotel, George Street, Marylebone, W1H 5JB; 020 7935 8131; www.durrantshotel.co.uk)

Durrants, run by the Miller family since 1921, is one of those rare hotels that really feel like home – especially if you happen to live in a posh country house. If you can't afford a room, sink into a leather armchair at the George Bar, a cocoon of gentility that's made for malt whiskies and the Sunday papers. It's like a miniature gentlemen's club with an open fire and judicious bartenders.

WINDSOR CASTLE

27–29 Crawford Place, Marylebone, W1H 4LJ
• 020 7723 4371
• Open Mon–Sat 11am–midnight, Sun 11am–11pm. Food served Mon–Fri & Sun noon–3pm and 6–10pm, Sat 6–10pm
• Transport Edgware Road tube
• Moderate

Royal regalia and furry fraternising

Republicans will be appalled by London's most royalist watering hole. The clue is in the name: this pub is a shrine to the House of Windsor. A life-size replica of a Foot Guard in a bearskin helmet stands guard in a sentry box outside. The windows are crammed with toby jugs, the walls are lined with coats of arms, and even the ceiling is covered in souvenir plates of the royal family. Among the portraits of countless royals are signed photos of soap stars and celebrities, from George Best to Pierce Brosnan.

This eye-popping collection of royal memorabilia was amassed by former landlord Michael Tierney, who isn't even British – he's a hard-drinking Irishman from Galway. (Apparently, Tierney drives a black cab, so he can drink and drive without getting busted.) Tierney retired in November 2010. The new landlady is Heather Robinson, a brassy blonde who hopefully has the sense not to change a thing.

The bar is lined with plaques dedicated to former and current regulars. One is "Reserved for Tom and John, celebrating 21 years of being 'civil' to each other". Another is reserved for the Handlebar Club of Great Britain, whose hirsute members gather here on the first Friday of every month, cheerfully slurping cocktail sausages, cucumber sandwiches and pints of bitter between their chops. Most are dressed in "member's regalia" – maroon silk ties and matching sweaters emblazoned with a white moustache. Prospective members must have "a hirsute appendage of the upper lip, with graspable extremities". The other essential qualification is "to be able to drink plenty of beer" and to engage in "furry fraternising", which involves frequent toasts "to the last whisker!" Apparently, members do occasionally engage in charitable stunts, such as finding out how many moustaches fit into a Mini.

Upstairs is a hidden dining room. Instead of steak and kidney pie, as you'd expect, on the menu is pad Thai. As the sign says: "The Queen was amused to hear that we're doing Thai food at the Windsor Castle." The obligatory portrait of Thailand's royal couple hangs above the door; otherwise the room is devoted to mugshots of a scowling Queen Victoria, jigsaw puzzles of the Queen Mother, and paparazzi shots of Princess Diana. The food is sanitised for Western palates, without the customary chilli kick, but the pad Thai and Keng Phed curry are both delicious. And they do serve fish and chips for die-hard traditionalists.

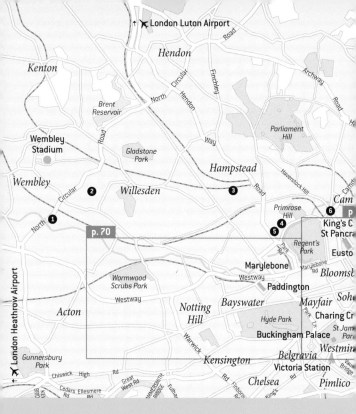

NORTH WEST, NORTH, NORTH EAST & EAST

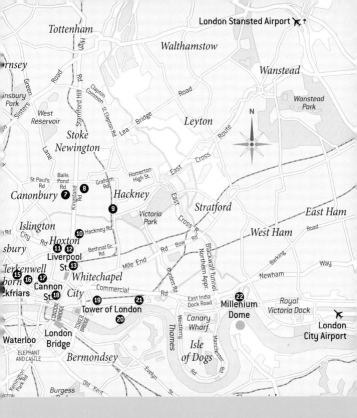

ACE CAFÉ ❶

Ace Corner, North Circular Road, Stonebridge, NW10 7UD
• 020 8961 1000
• www.ace-cafe-london.com
• Open Mon–Sat 7am–11pm (7am–2am when operating as a nightclub),
Sun & public holidays 7am–10.30pm
• Transport Stonebridge Park tube
• Moderate

Better than Little Chef

"Mostly we host petrol," says Mark Wilsmore. "On a warm night, there might be 5,000 bikes parked outside." For a man whose twin obsessions are motorbikes and rock and roll, Wilsmore has a dream job. He runs the Ace Café, a classic pit stop built in 1938 to cater for drivers using the new North Circular Road. A glamorous precursor of the motorway service station, there were petrol pumps, a "washmobile" that cost a whopping five shillings, car showrooms, and a restaurant, where football teams who played at Wembley ate after a match. Greasy truck drivers would refuel at the café next door.

Bombed during the war, the Ace Café was rebuilt in 1949. Open 24 hours, it soon became a magnet for teenage bikers who raced up and down the motorway. There was no speed limit in those days; daredevils would drop a

coin into the jukebox and race to a given point before the song ended. Rock and roll was banned from radios in the 1950s, so the Ace's jukebox was an attraction in its own right. (Sadly, the jukebox now reflects modern bikers' fondness for rock and metal.) "It was the birth of youth culture," says Wilsmore. "But they didn't serve booze back then, only mugs of strong tea and doorstop sandwiches."

The Ace Café closed in 1969. Subsequently used as a filling station, bookmaker, and tyre depot, the building remained pretty much intact. When Wilsmore organised a reunion in 1994 over 12,000 people turned up. He set up a burger shack on site, eventually bought the freehold and reopened the café in 1997.

Today, the setting – on a busy stretch of motorway opposite an industrial estate – doesn't exactly ooze glamour. Back then, the whole area would have reeked of vinegar from the Heinz factory nearby. Now, it smells of biscuits baking at the McVitie's factory. Yet nostalgic rockers, bikers, mods and Teddy boys continue to flock to this vintage-themed greasy spoon and "one-stop rockers' shop". Ageing rockabillies in leather jackets and greying quiffs come for the Gene Vincent and Eddie Cochran tribute bands. One day, the forecourt will be inundated with bearded beefcakes on Harleys, the next with sharply dressed mods and vintage Minis.

"The Ace has an almost religious significance for many people from all different demographics," says Wilsmore. "The bikes and the music may have changed, but the spirit remains the same."

SHAYONA ❷

54–62 Meadow Garth, Neasden, NW10 8HD
• 020 8965 3365
• www.shayonarestaurants.com
• Open Mon–Fri 11.30am–10pm, Sat, Sun 11am–10pm (last orders 9.30pm). The temple is open 7am–11.45pm and 4–8.30pm.
• Transport 15–20 min walk from Stonebridge Park, Neasden or Harlesden tube
• Budget

Palate cleanser

There's one very good reason to make a pilgrimage to Neasden, surely one of London's dreariest suburbs. Shri Swaminarayan Mandir, the largest Hindu temple outside India, is as much a tribute to Indian stonemasonry as to its spiritual guru, Bhagwan Swaminarayan. No metal was used in the temple's construction, only marble, limestone and wood. For two years, over 1,500 Indian craftsmen worked night and day to sculpt the seven pinnacles, six domes, and 26,300 pieces of intricately carved stone. Every piece was numbered and shipped in 160 containers to London, where the temple was assembled like a giant jigsaw puzzle.

A spry 98-year-old volunteer was on cloakroom duty when I visited. He was the perfect poster-boy for following a *sattvic* diet, which eschews spicy, salty and pungent foods such as onions and garlic, on the grounds that they agitate

the mind, causing lust and cravings for material possessions. Easy to digest, *sattvic* foods are said to purify the mind and body, bringing a sense of clarity, compassion and contentment. (Paul McCartney ordered *sattvic* snacks for his wedding to Heather Mills, but judging by their acrimonious divorce this didn't have the desired effect.)

Shayona, a charitable restaurant that raises funds for the temple and Hindu community, is the only pure *sattvic* restaurant in London. Across the road and through the temple car park, the entrance is via an Indian food store, with a mind-boggling array of (suspiciously spicy) Bombay mix and frozen pakoras. Beyond the day-glo sweet counter is a large dining room with an all-you-can-eat buffet. The back room is more formal, with wood-panelled walls, fake flowers, and a menu that covers the sub-continent.

Well-fed Indian families were tucking into Gujurati *thalis* and Keralan *dosas* on a midweek afternoon. (Weekends are busiest, both in the restaurant and temple.) There's no alcohol, only fresh juices or delicious mango lassi. Starters of samosas, bhajias and bel puris tend towards the deep-fried. A selection of dishes from Northern India was equally rich: Shayona Shahi Paneer (cheese in creamy saffron sauce), Dal Makhani (a beautifully buttery blend of mixed pulses), and Shayona Jeera (cumin rice), all scooped up with ghee-soaked nan bread.

According to *sattvic* principles, meals should be eaten between sunrise and sunset and you should only fill three-quarters of your stomach, leaving space for water and air. I certainly hadn't left any room for sweet *gulabjambus* and *rassomalais*, drenched in syrup and condensed milk.

Time your visit to coincide with evening prayers in the mandir, when monks chant mesmerising mantras before their idols, whose elaborate outfits are changed several times a day.

CZECH AND SLOVAK CLUB

74 West End Lane, West Hampstead, NW6 2LX
- 020 7372 1193
- www.czechoslovak-restaurant.co.uk
- Open Tues—Fri 5—11pm, Sat noon—11pm, Sun noon—10.30pm
- Transport West Hampstead tube
- Budget

Cholesterol check

I n 1939, the Duke of Bedford inaugurated a servicemen's club in Holborn for the Czechoslovakian legionaries who flew with the RAF to free Europe from Nazi occupation. In 1946, "due to the slight inconvenience regarding a ban for serving beer in Holborn", the legionaries sensibly relocated to a townhouse in leafy West Hampstead, purchased with their own savings and a £3,000 donation from the Czech President, Edvard Beneš. One of Beneš' former bodyguards, Martin Barančice, served as governor of Czechoslovak National House until his death aged 94. He was still pulling pints of Budvar in the bar in his nineties.

The spirit of the legionaries lives on at this delightful relic, pickled like sauerkraut, impervious to passing time. An evening here is like travelling to Eastern Europe before the Iron Curtain came down. (The club also served as a refuge for the new wave of migrants from Czechoslovakia during the Communist era.) There are threadbare carpets, burgundy drapes, brocade wallpaper and random portraits of the Pope, the Queen and various fighter pilots. It's all pleasantly down-at-heel.

There's no truck with faddish food trends either. On the menu are gargantuan portions of undeniably authentic but unremittingly stodgy Czech food. There are dumplings and pancakes, brawn and wild boar, fried goose liver with onions, potato noodles, and schnitzels the size of a small country. Most dishes are slathered in cream, cheese, breadcrumbs, or all three. Vegetarian options aren't exactly health-conscious either: deep-fried brie in breadcrumbs comes with chips. Langoš – deep-fried flatbread topped with garlic, cheddar, ketchup and tartare sauce – sounded like a heart attack on a plate.

We plumped for a comforting chicken broth with noodles and crispy potato pancakes, scattered with raw onions rather than sour cream. I guess they would taste great after several pints of the superlative lager available "on drought". Huge slabs of succulent meat came with "dumplings" that were more like slices of spongy white bread – great for mopping up the rich goulash sauce and sweet, sloppy sauerkraut. Thankfully, I ordered a half portion of goulash although the slim waiter assured me he could easily eat two portions in a single sitting.

We gawped at the homesick Slovaks and voracious Australians tackling the puddings – apricot dumplings, apple strudel or chocolate pancakes, all smothered in whipped cream – then retired to the bar to watch football, vowing to return in warmer weather to enjoy the secret beer garden.

OSLO COURT

4

Charlbert Street, St John's Wood, NW8 7EN
- 020 7722 8795
- Open Mon–Sat noon–2.30pm and 7–11pm, closed Sun and all August
- Transport St John's Wood tube
- Expensive

In the pink

Student digs aren't what they used to be. Most of the £400,000 flats in Oslo Court are occupied by international students, who enjoy stunning views of Regent's Park and easy access to one of London's most surreal restaurants.

Oslo Court is a 1970s' theme park trapped inside a 1930s' tower block. The restaurant has no sign, no website, and has never advertised. But on Friday lunchtime, the place is packed with birthday parties, bar mitzvahs, and blue rinses.

After some confusion with our reservation ("Your name is Gaul? Paul? Ah, Hall!"), we were ushered in by a solicitous waiter. The flouncy pink interior is like a paean to the prawn cocktail – a popular fixture on the vast set menu. You can mix and match from dozens of starters, mains and endless specials that never seem to change. Every dish is a throwback: grilled pink grapefruit with brown sugar and sherry, beef Wellington, steak Diane, duckling crisp with cherry sauce, and alarming combinations such as seafood crepe with cheese sauce.

Prices are fixed, but like a Jewish matriarch, they ply you with colossal portions until you're at bursting point. First there are crudités with mayonnaise and warm buttered rolls, a tureen of fish soup, followed by a whole Dover sole and heaps of vegetables. Only the Melba toasts, which taste like leathery slippers, are disappointing.

Spanish brothers Tony and José Sanchez have run the place since 1982 along with their extended family. Our Portuguese waiter's staccato delivery was disconcerting ("Grillfryorpoach? Oilanlemonwhitewineancream-sauceorgarlicbutter? Sautéeboilchipsormash?"), but service is fantastically efficient and comes with lashings of banter. José works the room, introducing himself with the unforgettable line: "My wife is married, but I'm single."

When the dessert waiter minces over, bursting out of his embellished waistcoat, we protest that we are too full. "Come on, Dad!" he says to my younger date. "Just a coupla raspberries? Pieca pavlova to take home?" Neil ("I think it's a stage name – he's Russian," the owner's vivacious daughter Maria Sanchez confides) has been acting the part for over three decades.

Many guests are still wrapping up lunch when the dinner service begins. The whole room bursts into song when a birthday cake is wheeled out. The Oslo Court experience is like being an extra in a *Carry On* film. Although my companion complained that he felt as if he'd "just swallowed a packet of butter", I left feeling buoyant, delighted that such stalwarts can thrive in fashion- and calorie-conscious London. Anyway, you can walk off the butter with a stroll through Regent's Park. Don't forget to take those Melba toasts to feed the ducks.

CAB SHELTERS ⑤

Locations: Chelsea Embankment (near Albert Bridge), SW3;
Embankment Place, Charing Cross, WC2; Grosvenor Gardens, Victoria,
SW1; Hanover Square, Mayfair, W1; Kensington Park Road, Notting Hill,
W11; Kensington Road (north side), South Kensington, W8; Pont Street,
Belgravia, SW1; Russell Square (west corner), Bloomsbury, WC1; St
George's Square, Pimlico, SW1; Temple Place, Victoria Embankment,
WC2; Thurloe Place, South Kensington, SW7; Clifton Gardens, Maida Vale,
W9; Wellington Place, St John's Wood, NW8
• Budget

The cheapest taxi fare in town

London's characteristic black cabs are the direct descendants of the London Hackney Carriage, first licensed by an act of Oliver Cromwell in June 1654. Taxis were built with high roofs so that their illustrious clientele didn't have to remove their top hats. However, not all passengers were well bred: in 1694, some lady passengers behaved so badly in a cab near Hyde Park that the authorities banned cabs from the park for the next 230 years.

All of London's cab drivers are required to have "the Knowledge". This exam, introduced in 1865, means cabbies must remember every street within

6 miles of Charing Cross (the official centre of London). This formidable feat can take three years to achieve and only about half of all trainees pass.

Originally, cab drivers weren't allowed to leave their vehicles when parked, so in 1874 the Earl of Shaftesbury set up the Cabmen's Shelter Fund to construct and run roadside huts to provide cabbies with "good and wholesome refreshments at moderate prices". The result was a flourishing of green wooden sheds around the capital. Because the shelters stand directly on a public highway, they could be no bigger than a horse and cart. Even so, they still manage to squeeze in a working kitchen and space for over ten men. The philanthropists who set up the shelters were typically high-minded Victorians: gambling, drinking, swearing and talking politics were strictly forbidden. The original intention in getting the cabmen into the shelters was not only to feed them, but also to keep them out of the pub.

There were originally 61 of these shelters, but numbers have dwindled to 13. The few remaining sheds, often in some of the poshest parts of London, are now listed buildings. Thankfully, they still thrive as a place for colleagues to meet and eat. Only cabbies are allowed to sit inside, but anyone can get a take-away – "bacon roll, brown sauce, tea, three sugars, thanks love" – through the serving hatch. The menu is generally basic fare such as sausage rolls and ham and cheese sandwiches, although some shelters will knock up a full English breakfast. Prices are dirt-cheap, but sweet-toothed patrons might be penalised: "Please note if you would like 4-5-6 sugars in your tea or coffee, you will be charged 5p extra."

NICE GREEN CAFÉ   ❻

Cecil Sharp House, 2 Regent's Park Road, Camden, NW1 7AY
- 07779 026052
- www.efdss.org
- Open 10am–7.30pm daily, open later for evening concerts and events
- Transport Camden Town or Chalk Farm tube
- Budget

Cakes and ceilidhs

" **I**t will be all Morris dancing and wholemeal bicycles," my lunch companion warned as we approached Cecil Sharp House, home to the English Folk Dance and Song Society. The 1930s' brick building, with a pretty walled garden originally designed as an open-air theatre, is easy to miss. Inside, the rehearsal rooms were abustle with excitable drama students and hirsute musicians. Classes and events cover everything from Appalachian clogging to barn dancing and bluegrass bands. One regular describes the Friday night ceilidhs as "bedlam".

A big band was rehearsing in the Kennedy Hall; we peeked inside to admire the 70-foot Ivon Hitchens mural of folk dancers frolicking in an Arcadian landscape. The billowing chorus followed us downstairs to the basement café, where teenagers in legwarmers were tucking into brie and apple sandwiches. All pastels and polka dots, vintage teapots and cake stands, it looked like the Fame school redesigned by Cath Kidston. With a counter strung with bunting and crockery in treacle tins, it's suitably folksy without being too twee.

Manager Helen Tindale taught cooking at schools and sold organic ice cream from her Nice Green Van before setting up shop here in September 2010. As well as sandwiches, sausage rolls and pies, there are three or four specials that change every day. Thick sweet potato and carrot soup and a comforting chickpea stew were served with brown rolls still warm from the oven. Ingredients are carefully sourced and mostly organic. Tindale has revived the kitchen garden planted during the Second World War. Beer and wine are served when the real ale bar next door is closed. And there's always a selection of cakes. "When a 150-strong orchestra comes in, you really don't want to run out of cake," says Tindale.

Despite the vast quantities of cake consumed, it's more of a social enterprise than a profitable business. Helen's 8-year-old son Fabian helps bake biscuits after school – but then gives them all away. 10p from every drink is donated to the café's Meals on Wheels service, which delivers hot meals to housebound residents by bicycle. Not wholemeal ones, mind you.

NEARBY

FERREIRA DELICATESSEN

(40 Delancey Street, Camden, NW1 7RY; 020 7485 2351)

Every lunchtime, a queue snakes out of this friendly corner shop. The crowds come for the giant sandwiches stuffed with Portuguese delicacies from the deli counter: *ilha* cheese from the Azores, spicy salamis and smoked *chouriço*. And divine custard tarts, of course.

HUONG VIET

12–14 Englefield Road, Dalston, N1 4LS
• 020 7249 0877
• Open Mon–Sat noon–3.30pm, 5.30–11pm
• Transport Dalston Kingsland rail
• Budget

Soup kitchen for thick skins

Hoxton has a reputation for silly haircuts, modelled after indie rockers and fashion-conscious footballers. Much of the blame for these fins and faux-hawks lies with the Vietnamese beauty parlours that have sprung up along Kingsland Road, beside the neon-bright canteens that serve steaming bowls of *pho* for a song.

But the real culprit is Khanh Thanh Vu, director of the An Viet foundation, set up in 1982 to provide practical help and vocational training for Vietnamese refugees fleeing the Communist regime. Mr Vu was one of the original "boat people" granted asylum in Britain in the late '70s. Many of them settled in Hackney, where rents were cheap and squats abundant. Initially, the Vietnamese community worked mainly in the local textile industry, but soon developed a niche in no-frills restaurants and beauty salons.

Mr Vu's wife runs Huong Viet, a restaurant in the An Viet centre, with part of the proceeds going to support community projects. By day, it's easy to bypass the run-down building, formerly a public laundry and bathhouse. At night, a throng of hopefuls squeezes into the dimly lit vestibule, poring over the perplexing selection of noodles, curries, sizzling meats and hot and sour soups. I lived around the corner for a while, but despite regular visits didn't manage to sample more than a fraction of the menu. That's because I couldn't resist ordering the same chef's specials: crisp summer rolls with plum sauce, crunchy char-grilled squid, whole steamed sea bass with ginger and garlic, *banh xeo* (an oversized pancake stuffed with chicken, prawns and spicy stir-fried vegetables), and beef salad with vermicelli, mint, lemongrass and chilli.

I've had some awful meals at feted establishments on Kingsland Road, but despite mixed reviews from other visitors I've never had a bad experience at Huong Viet. It's dirt-cheap and you can bring your own booze.

An Viet means "well settled", but dining here can be an unsettling experience – partly because of the wobbly chairs, tiny tables jammed together, dreadful acoustics and dubious cleanliness, but mostly on account of the comically brusque service. The rudeness of the staff has acquired cult status. They wilfully ignore you, bring the wrong dishes at random intervals, mutter abuse if you complain, and are generally more concerned with maintaining their asymmetrical hairstyles and dazzling manicures than serving you. Weekends are crammed, so book ahead or, better still, go midweek.

LMNT

316 Queensbridge Road, Dalston, E8 3NH
• 020 7249 6727
• www.lmnt.co.uk
• Open Mon—Thurs 6—11pm, Fri, Sat noon—11pm, Sun noon—10.30pm
• Transport Dalston Junction or Haggerston Overground, bus 149, 242, 30, 38, 56, 19, 236
• Moderate

> *London's most eccentric dining room*

It's not often that you arrive at a rendezvous to find your dinner date seated inside a giant urn. But that's what happened when I showed up at LMNT on a Saturday night. I clambered inside the candlelit pot. It was stuffy and our conversation punctuated by the constant clatter of pans from the nearby kitchen. Other seating arrangements are equally odd. Some diners were squeezed into operatic boxes high up in the corners of the room, others in sunken booths or a wooden balcony built above the bar.

When the previous owner, Peter Ilic, bought the place in 2000 it was a rundown pub in a desolate corner of Dalston, long before the area was overrun with organic coffee shops and artists' collectives. "It was the middle of nowhere. Taxi drivers wouldn't even come here," says Dragan, the gruff new owner.

Ilic figured the only way to bring in the punters would be to make the decor as outrageous as possible. Billing itself as "London's most eccentric dining room", the place is a pastiche of Roman, Greek, Mesopotamian, and Egyptian imagery. A fireplace sputters inside a giant Sphinx; a gold bust is draped in faux bijoux; Jesus gazes down on diners from one side of the room, Tutankhamen on the other. Orgiastic scenes are plastered all over the bathrooms, where tittering teenagers were taking pictures with their smartphones. In the ladies' loos, you're greeted by a statuesque nude jerking off and a grinning devil whose (amazingly still erect) member is being amputated with a hot poker.

Judging by our fellow diners, LMNT is popular for birthday parties and blind dates. Prices are keen, cheaper still at lunchtime, but the food is less memorable than the surroundings. A fatty ham hock terrine overloaded with oregano proved inedible. Three soggy slices of speck were wrapped around limp lettuce leaves, garnished with orange slices (not the advertised blood oranges). Main courses were better, but tender lamb in a red wine reduction was marred by an accompaniment of tinned beans; smoked haddock by a lumpy pillow of bubble and squeak (actually just rehashed mash potato). They'd forgotten to put the dates in the sticky toffee pudding.

The Slavic school of service – which Dragan unapologetically defined as "my way or the highway" – leaves much to be desired. No questions were asked when dishes were left half eaten. "I wouldn't come back for the food," my companion admitted. "But to experience this interior once is worth the trip." She lives up the road in Stoke Newington, so I'm not sure this is a ringing endorsement.

PLATFORM

Studio 207, Netil House, 1–7 Westgate Street, London Fields, E8 3RL
- 020 3095 9713 (buzz 207 for entry if there's nobody on the door)
- www.platformlondonfields.com
- Open Mon–Thurs 8.30am–8pm, Fri 8.30am–1am, Sat 4pm–1am
- Transport Bus 55, London Fields Overground
- Moderate (cash only)

*Room
with a view*

We accidentally stumbled into a photo shoot while looking for this well-hidden staff canteen that morphs into a bar at weekends. Wedged between Broadway Market and Mare Street, Netil House is a drab 1960's office block that was a community college, council offices and a squat before it became derelict for over a decade. The entrance to Platform café, via a grubby alleyway alongside a railway bridge, doesn't bode well either. But appearances can be deceptive.

Platform is not your typical staff cafeteria, but the residents of Netil House are not your typical office workers. Pilates instructors, tattoo artists, illustrators and acrobats inhabit the studios leading off the green linoleum staircase, the last vestige of the building's institutional past. You can peek into the artists' studios during the day, or pretend you're one of them in the second floor café. It's an unexpectedly huge space with scuffed concrete floors, a mash up of vintage furniture, and a wall of windows overlooking the East London skyline. There's Canary Wharf to the left, the Gherkin and the Shard to your right. Sunsets from the terrace overlooking London Fields are spectacular. Trains chugging along the railway tracks at eye level give the scene a faintly futuristic edge.

There's a relaxed, improvised feel to everything from the sexy young staff to the simple, affordable food. The daily changing menu contains half a dozen dishes, all produced in a tiny kitchen beside the bar. There are wholesome vegetarian options such as roast butternut and ginger soup or green lentil, date and roast pepper salad, and occasionally inspired snacks – crayfish and olive *bruschetta* in a sour cream and paprika dressing and a roasted vegetable sandwich with grilled *paneer* marinated in saffron and lemon zest.

Acoustic music tinkles from the stack of speakers by day. The beats get louder by night, as Hackney's finest come to share gossip and cheap drinks on battered leather sofas and Formica tables. There's a piano in one corner for impromptu singalongs, but there are planned events too, from film nights to ping-pong tournaments and occasional rooftop parties.

NEARBY

WILTON WAY CAFÉ

(63 Wilton Way, London Fields, E8 1BG; www.londonfieldsradio.com/café)
London Fields Radio broadcasts live from a radio booth in the corner of this cute café, where all the furniture is fashioned from crates and corrugated iron.

YE OLDE AXE ⑩

69 Hackney Road, Shoreditch, E2 8ET
• 020 7729 5137
• Open Greasy Rock n Roll every Saturday midnight–6am
• Transport Old Street or Liverpool Street tube
• Moderate

Stripped down swing

You don't want to come to this Shoreditch boozer at the wrong time of day. I stumbled in on a Friday afternoon and came face to face with a (not particularly pert) pair of butt cheeks. A few slack-jawed, pot-bellied men were drooling into warm pints, while lithe young ladies pole-danced around them. I stumbled straight out again.

Ye Olde Axe is one of the last traditional strip pubs in the East End, although Browns, its flashier rival a few doors down, seems to be packing in the punters, its hefty bouncers flanked by fake flaming torches. Browns might have bling, but it doesn't have the Axe's decadent Victorian interiors: sticky leather love seats, an even stickier carpet, a gilt-panelled ceiling, and an ornate wooden bar. Even the scuffed poles in the centre of the room are topped with golden flourishes.

Around midnight on Saturdays, Ye Olde Axe is a very different proposition. As the girls inside get dressed, a queue of guys and dolls dressed to kill is forming outside. They are here for Greasy Rock n Roll, a frenzied rockabilly party that starts at midnight and doesn't stop until 6am. The dress code is 1950s' retro. There are fantastic frocks, gleaming quiffs, tattoos aplenty, and some very nifty footwork on the dance floor. Service is gruff (no wonder, with such a crush), drinks are served in plastic cups, and the grubby toilets reek of unrequited lust, but you're guaranteed to be dancing until dawn.

As you stagger out into the grey morning light, don't bother checking the triple-faced clock tower that crowns the red-brick building: the clocks stopped long ago. According to *The Haunted Pub Guide*, the site holds another unsavoury secret. In 1979 a team of workmen were renovating the pub, which had been derelict for twenty-five years. While digging the foundations, they unearthed the legs and skulls of two decomposed bodies, buried with a rusty pair of scissors.

NEARBY

GEORGE & DRAGON

(2–4 Hackney Road, E2 7NS; 020 7012 1100; www.whitecubicle.org)
At this raucous gay bar, the ladies' loos have been converted into the White
Cubicle gallery – an ironic antidote to the po-faced White Cube nearby. The
toilet is a grotty backdrop for site-specific art, which tends to be camp, kitsch
and erotically charged. Exhibition openings are a riot, with performances by
drag queen DJs, go-go boys or guacamole chefs.

LOUNGE BOHEMIA

1e Great Eastern Street, Shoreditch, EC2A 3EJ
- 07720 707000
- www.loungebohemia.com
- Open Mon–Sat 6pm–midnight, Sun 6pm–11pm
- Transport Old Street tube
- Moderate

*Underground
paean
to mid-century
modern*

I t takes brass to call a kebab shop the Savoy and it takes a bold bartender to create a cocktail bar that's by appointment only. Paul Tvaroh's Lounge Bohemia is hidden in a basement below the Corner Savoy takeaway, but you won't get in without calling ahead. The "no standing, no suits" policy means that it's never crowded and the clientele is infallibly cool.

The bearded, brooding Tvaroh, who really is from Bohemia in the Czech Republic, spent months searching for a venue. "I noticed the shutters one day and wondered what was on the other side … It was an abandoned Chinese restaurant with some very scary-looking ingredients that had been left behind. It took a lot of TLC to get it to where it is now."

A barely lit corridor plastered with Czech newspapers leads to a secret lair dedicated to molecular mixology and mid-century modern design. The bar is constructed from furniture that belonged to Tvaroh's grandmother. Menus are hidden in vintage hardbacks, prohibition style. While you investigate the intriguing cocktail list, the waitress brings a trio of unusual canapés (perhaps a prune wrapped in peppered ham or cod roe mousse crumpet). The swing soundtrack is never too loud – this is a place for serious conversation as well as seriously experimental drinkers.

There's absinthe in various guises and a long line of Czech lagers, liquors and homemade eaux de vie. It's probably the only place in London where you'll find kosher slivovice (plum brandy). But the real draw is Tvaroh's extraordinary selection of in-house syrups and infusions, which form the basis of his own brand of "manipulative mixology". There's Stolichnaya vodka infused with poppy seed or porcini, bourbon infused with black forest ham, and Cuban rum infused with a Romeo & Juliet cigar. Syrups are flavoured with Jack Daniel's oak barrel chippings, cinnamon bark and parma violet.

Molecular cocktails are as much about overturning expectation as theatrical presentation. Holy Smoke (leather infused cognac, frankincense and myrrh smoke, served in a gold glass holder) was inspired by the three kings and their gifts. Afternoon Tree is an elaborate candyfloss sculpture made from crystallised becherovka, a Czech digestive liqueur with spicy undertones of cloves and cinnamon. "Everyone expects the candyfloss to be very sweet, when in fact it's quite bitter with a kick to it," says Tvaroh. "Now I have the only bar in London where the candyfloss machine takes pride of place. My wife calls me obsessive; I'd call it a healthy love of the job."

TIME FOR TEA

110 Shoreditch High St, Shoreditch, E1 6JN
- 020 3222 0073
- Open Sun 2pm–7pm (Opening times are erratic, so do call ahead)
- Transport Old Street or Liverpool Street tube
- Budget

Putting on the Blitz

"Are you here for tea and cake?" asks the gentleman with the impressive soup strainer. With his high-waisted trousers, braces and severe side parting, he looks as though he's just stepped out of a Graham Greene novel. The green and grey parlour is also straight out of the 1940s: a portrait of King George VI hangs above an antique piano and a Norton motorbike is parked beside a vintage jukebox that plays wartime swing.

If this vintage tearoom feels like someone's front room, that's because it is. But it's no ordinary home. It's a recreation 1940s' townhouse belonging to Johnny Vercoutre, a club promoter, art director and vintage obsessive – who is also my waiter today. It took him three years to restore the five-storey building, a printer's warehouse that had been derelict since 1942, to its original state. He scoured auctions, markets and antique shops for period bathtubs, tiles and wallpaper. Johnny's Great Dane prowls among the period props, all of which are for hire. The house is often used for TV and fashion shoots, and the parlour doubles as a screening room. For private parties, Johnny spins 78 records on the gramophone.

On Sundays, Johnny and his equally dapper sidekick, Graham Hilleard, open the front room to serve afternoon tea to friends and curious passers-by. In the tiny kitchen, rows of vintage tins are labelled with exotic teas. Johnny's mum, Lulu, makes the delicious banana, carrot and orange cakes lined up on the wooden counter. For a more traditional option, order scones with clotted cream and cucumber sandwiches, all served on mismatched vintage china. With only a handful of tables, you might end up sharing your pot of tea with strangers.

"I called the house Time for Tea because it came with a clock on the front, and I wanted to revive the British institution of afternoon tea," says Johnny. The original clock on the shop front doesn't tell the time: it doesn't have any hands. It's a fitting marker for a place where time seems to have stood still. In any case, it's always time for tea.

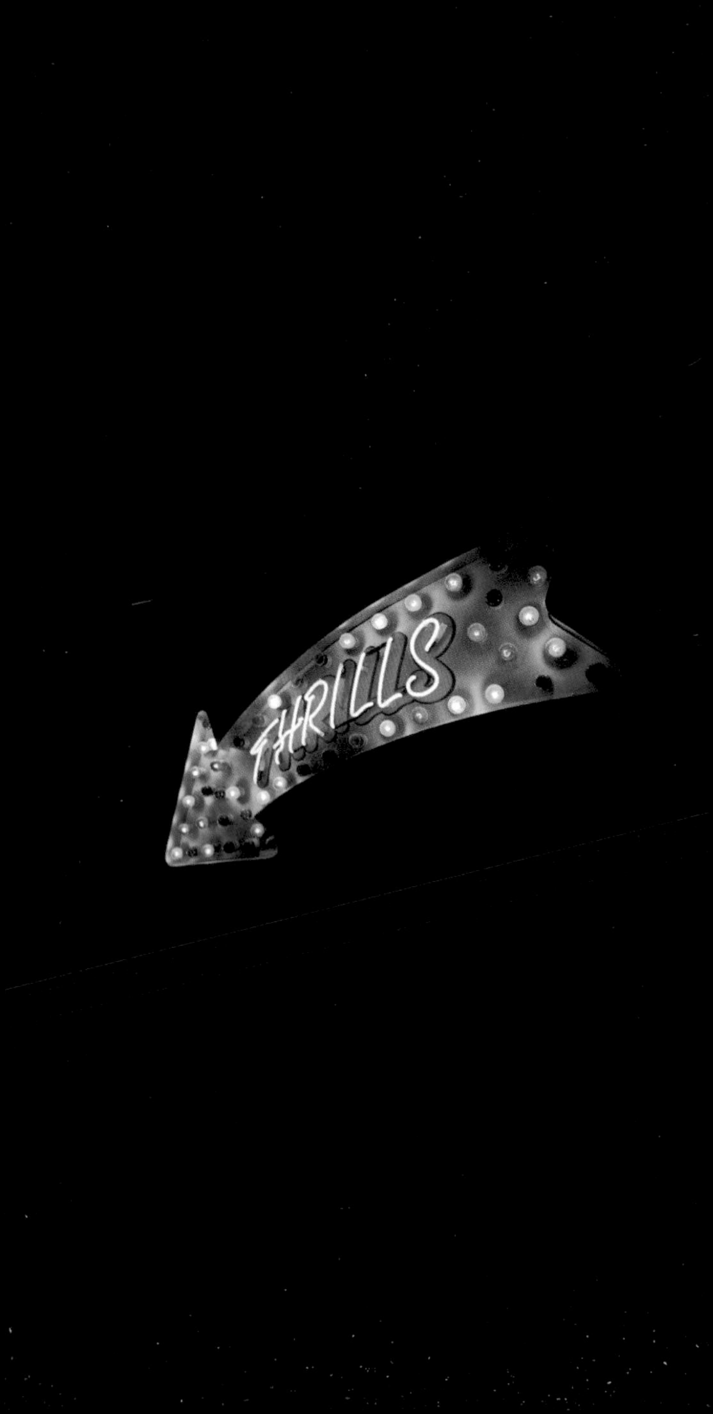
THRILLS

THE MAYOR OF SCAREDY CAT TOWN

12–16 Artillery Lane, Spitalfields, E1 7LS
- 020 7078 9639
- www.themayorofscaredycattown.com
- Open Mon–Thurs 5pm–midnight (last entry 11pm), Fri, Sat noon–midnight, Sun noon–10.30pm
- Transport Liverpool Street tube/rail
- Moderate

Ask
to see
The Mayor

Every speakeasy in London claims to have been inspired by Please Don't Tell in New York's East Village, accessed via a vintage phone booth in a hot dog joint. The Mayor of Scaredy Cat Town doesn't pretend to be a speakeasy, but its entrance is equally unusual: through a white Smeg fridge inside the Spitalfields branch of The Breakfast Club.

Skip the queue for French toast and tell one of the staff you're here to see The Mayor. Beyond the fridge door is a dark staircase with a neon arrow flashing "Thrills". The small basement bar is a cosy, dimly lit nook of exposed brick and kitsch Americana. A stuffed moose head is draped in a lei; a pimped-up portrait of the Queen sports real sunglasses and rapper chains. A door signposted "the second smallest disco in the world" leads to the loos: a homage to the 1980s, plastered in a Smash Hits collage featuring Paul Young and Samantha Fox.

Apparently, the bar's name came from an episode of *Cheers*. The management have taken the branding a little too far by calling the bar snacks "Cat Food". The menu, stuffed into a cat food tin, is a catalogue of guilty pleasures – chilli cheese chips, buffalo wings and blue cheese – designed to appeal to people who've had too many of the delicious chilli and lemongrass margaritas. Other notable house cocktails are Rosie and Gin (Bombay Sapphire, pineapple juice, rosemary and lime) and Basil-no-Faulty (vodka, elderflower liqueur, fresh basil and lime). There's table service so you never have to fight for a refill. With a maximum capacity of 60, they don't take reservations except for brunch.

The weekend brunch menu (served until 4pm and groaningly dubbed "The Hair of the Cat") is especially appealing if you're recovering from the night before. Poached egg on toast with avocado, bacon, and chilli hits the spot. An unlikely combination of pancakes with bacon, blueberries and maple syrup is strangely good. The biggest draw is the DIY Bloody Mary bar, with a choice of dozens of ingredients including bacon and pickled ginger mixed with homemade roasted cherry tomato juice.

Patrons are requested to exit through the Breakfast Club toilets rather than the fridge, although don't take the house rules too seriously: "Gentlemen, you are advised to leave your fly down to add to the charade. Ladies, if you'd leave your skirt in your knickers, it would be greatly appreciated."

THE SIX CLERKS

113 Chancery Lane, WC2A 1PL
- 020 7316 5580
- Open Lunch Mon–Fri noon–14.30pm; Bar Mon–Fri noon–9.30pm
- Transport Chancery Lane tube
- Moderate

A courtly affair

Soliciting for sex might be a crime, but the solicitors who prosecute such misdemeanours are generally considered less than sexy. "Lawyers are no longer red-nosed, dribbling fuddy-duddies sitting by the fire with a pipe," insists Steve Matthews. And he should know: Matthews manages The Six Clerks restaurant, a discreet member's bar inside The Law Society, which opened to the public in November 2011.

"Before we renovated, it looked like a comfortable pair of slippers – now, we're showcasing the contemporary side of a very traditional building," says Matthews, as he surveys the boxy dining room, a vision of beige and brown. Personally, I'd prefer some cosy slippers to these shiny brogues, but the lunchtime clientele is certainly polished and relatively youthful.

In the heart of London's legal community, The Law Society's neo-Georgian HQ is sandwiched between the Old Bailey and the Inns of Court. Founded in 1825 to weed out the "pettifoggers and vipers" putting the profession to shame, today every solicitor practising in England and Wales has to be a member of The Law Society.

Once you get past security and are issued with a visitor's pass, it still has a clubby feel. Portraits of past presidents line the walls. A plaque commemorates the six clerks based here between 1511 and 1621, who acted as middlemen between the in-house attorneys and the courts. Their offices burned down after one of the clerics failed to clean the chimney. They rebuilt on the site of the present dining room and remained there until 1778. Eventually, they had to relocate after the weight of all their paperwork caused the floor to collapse.

The bar is open throughout the day, but lunch is the main event. The menu is clearly designed with business meetings in mind – all manly steaks, burgers and triple-decker club sandwiches. There are a few soups and salads for the fairer sex. (The first woman solicitor, Carrie Morrison, was admitted to The Law Society in 1922, after beating four other female contenders in a running race along Chancery Lane.) The food may be middle-of-the-road, but it's well executed. Warm rolls and caraway buns precede the bargain three-course set menu of brie, onion and tomato tartlet, seared red mullet with a crunchy accompaniment of carrot, parsnip and broad beans, and poached plums with mascarpone ice cream.

You can also take tea in the original Reading Room, surrounded by red marble columns and a dazzling sapphire and gold carpet – a far sexier space, in my view.

Ye Olde Mitre

OPEN
MON — FRIDAY
11 — 11pm

HOT + COLD FOOD
IS AVAILABLE
FROM 11·30 — 9·30PM
REAL ALES OUR
SPECIALITY

YE OLDE MITRE

1 Ely Court (entrance from Ely Place or between 9 & 10 Hatton Garden),
Farringdon, EC1N 6SJ
- 020 7405 4751
- Open Mon–Fri 11am–11pm
- Transport Chancery Lane or Farringdon tube
- Moderate

> **The most secret pub in Cambridgeshire**

" This is definitely London's most hidden pub," says John Wright, who has been serving pints of real ale and toasted cheese sandwiches at Ye Olde Mitre for 27 years. Technically, this pub isn't in London at all. Originally built in 1547 for the servants of Ely Palace, London seat of the Bishop of Ely, it's still officially part of Cambridgeshire. Back in those days, England's bishops all had a residence in London because they sat in Parliament. Ely Palace was one of the grandest, with fountains, vineyards and strawberry fields stretching as far as the Thames.

Today's incarnation of Ye Olde Mitre dates from 1772, soon after Ely Palace was demolished. The wonky little pub is hidden down an alley linking Ely Place, a gated Georgian cul-de-sac, and Hatton Garden, an enclave of Jewish diamond dealers. The latter is named after Christopher Hatton, a mover and shaker in the court of Elizabeth I. In 1576, Hatton sweet-talked the Queen into leasing him a large part of Ely Palace for a yearly rent of one red rose, ten loads of hay and £10. Hatton later became Lord Chancellor, but didn't manage his own finances very well: he died owing the Crown £40,000.

In the pub's firelit front parlour is the preserved trunk of a cherry tree, which marked the boundary between Hatton's and the Bishop's property. Allegedly, Elizabeth I performed the maypole dance around this tree. Wooden settles and Tudor portraits line the mahogany-panelled back room, which leads to Ye Closet, a snug that merits the name. Barrels are dotted around the cloistered courtyard, an oasis on summer nights. The menu is as traditional as the interior: sandwiches, sausages, gherkins, and a fine selection of ales.

Sadly, beadles no longer call the hours or light the street lamps, but licensing hours are still fixed to the closing of the gates on Ely Place, so Ye Olde Mitre is shut at weekends. Until 1978, London's police could only enter Ely Place by invitation. "Criminals would run down the alley because the coppers couldn't follow them," Wright recalls. "They'd have to lock the gates and wait for reinforcements from Cambridge."

NEARBY

CLOISTER CAFÉ
The only survivor of Ely Palace is St Etheldreda's, England's oldest Roman Catholic church, built in 1291. Unlike sleepy St Etheldreda's, the medieval church of St Bartholomew the Great in Smithfield is on the tourist trail. The gloomy café in the cloisters serves Trappist beer, best savoured in silence like the monks who produce it.

BREAKFAST AND BRUNCH BAR (COCK TAVERN)

East Poultry Avenue, Smithfield Market, Farringdon, EC1A 9LH
• 020 7236 4923
• Open Mon–Fri 6am–3pm
• Transport Farringdon tube
• Budget

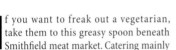

*Hold
the veg*

If you want to freak out a vegetarian, take them to this greasy spoon beneath Smithfield meat market. Catering mainly to foul-mouthed butchers in blood-spattered aprons in need of sustenance after a night shift, it serves London's most carnivorous breakfasts. And you can order a pint with your sausage, bacon, kidney, liver, black pudding, steak, egg and chips, even if it's only 6am. Named after its location inside the poultry market, the pub was originally called The Cock Tavern. Bizarrely, the owners recently changed the name to Breakfast and Brunch Bar; nothing else has changed, which makes the "rebrand" even more baffling. The stench of blood mingles with the smell of stale bacon fat as you cross the incongruous aluminium doorway and descend into the basement. It's a large, gloomy room with beige banquettes, Sky Sports on TV, and a pool table. Only the black and white photographs of the 800-year-old meat market create a sense of place.

I've never been able to muster the appetite for one of the Master Steaks, which come drenched in improbably posh sauces such as stilton and port or brie and spring onion. Breakfasts aren't sensational. A scalding plate of scrambled eggs and very salty bacon, served with bubble and squeak, a doorstep of toast, and a mug of extra strong tea would taste a lot better if you'd been up all night drinking or you'd spent the last six hours lugging carcasses.

The busiest time is between 6am and 8am. You might get the odd red-eyed clubber from Fabric (the nightclub nearby), but mostly it's butchers, builders, policemen, nurses and doctors winding down after working all night. The artist Lucian Freud was a regular; he loved the devilled kidneys. "He even did an interview with *Tatler* down here," recalls the affable manager John Fitzsimons, who has worked here for 25 years. A smattering of actors and aristocrats has visited over the years. On the morning of the 2001 elections, the Tory candidate William Hague came for breakfast – a desperate attempt to get down with the people. This gritty joint isn't for toffs. Fitzsimons nods: "We don't sell a lot of champagne breakfasts."

NEARBY

LE CAFÉ DU MARCHÉ
(Charterhouse Mews, 22 Charterhouse Square, Farringdon, EC1M 6DX; 020 7608 1609; www.cafedumarche.co.uk)
Hidden down a cobbled mews off Charterhouse Square, this *très* French restaurant has a loyal following. The set menu is hit-and-miss, but the authentically Gallic ambience is seductive. Le Grenier upstairs is perfect for clandestine trysts (and does excellent *frites*), occasionally accompanied by a jazz trio.

THE VIADUCT TAVERN

126 Newgate Street, The City of London, EC1A 7AA
- 020 7600 1863
- Open Mon–Fri 11am–11pm
- Transport St Paul's tube or City Thameslink rail
- Moderate

> *A jailhouse in a gin palace*

The Victorians were gluttons for punishment – capital crimes included impersonating an Egyptian, stealing an heiress, and poaching a rabbit; but they were also gluttons for gin. This 19th-century pub combines the two. The first public building in London equipped with electric lighting, the Viaduct Tavern is one of the city's last surviving gin palaces. These lavishly decorated boozers, where the upper classes mingled with low life, first appeared around 1830.

With its gold-edged mirrors and beaten copper ceiling, this pub is a typical example. The giant triptych represents the statues of Commerce, Agriculture, Science and Fine Arts on nearby Holborn Viaduct, which opened in 1869, the same year as the pub. (Look for the wound in Science's rump, pierced by a soldier's bayonet during celebrations to mark the end of the First World War.) The landlady would dispense gin tokens from the mahogany and etched-glass booth behind the bar. The pub still does a fine gin and tonic, with a choice of over ten gins.

However, the romantic interior doesn't prepare you for the horrors in the basement. The pub was built on the site of the Giltspur Comptor, a sheriff's office with a debtors' gaol affiliated to Newgate Prison. Little remains of this infamous prison, the city's main jail for almost five centuries. Originally located by a medieval gate in the Roman London Wall, it was demolished in 1902. The Central Criminal Courts now stand on the site.

If you ask nicely, the staff will show you five cells that survived the prison's closure, now used in part as beer cellars. Bitterly cold, damp and dark, the underground cells still look like the real deal. The ghost of a young prostitute supposedly haunts one cell, but visitors don't need to be psychic to sniff out the misery. Up to twenty criminals – men, women, children – and countless rats were crammed into each 12 by 8 feet cell. There was no toilet; one gaoler described the stench as "enough to turn the stomach of a horse". The only daylight was from a hole in the ceiling leading to street level, used by relatives or sympathetic passers-by to drop down scraps of food.

When I expressed horror at these conditions, the Polish waitress shrugged. "At least they wouldn't want to come back – now prison is like a hotel." Ironically, George Michael's *Freedom* was playing when we surfaced into the bar upstairs.

SIMPSON'S TAVERN

Ball Court, 38½ Cornhill, City of London, EC3V 9DR
• 020 7626 9985
• www.simpsonstavern.co.uk
• Open Mon–Fri noon–3pm; breakfast Tues–Fri 8–11am; bars 11.30am–3.30pm
• Transport Bank tube
• Moderate

Guess the stewed cheese

Chicken and ham pie on Monday, roast beef with Yorkshire pudding on Tuesday, baked ham with parsley sauce on Wednesday … If this sounds like your school dinner rota, don't be alarmed. The daily specials at Simpson's Tavern, which haven't changed for 250 years, are tastier than anything you were force-fed at school. If you want to ring the changes, there's plenty more "good honest fare": chump chops, bubble and squeak, stilton and tawny port for dessert. The house speciality, "Stewed Cheese", isn't on the menu. A hot pot of melted, mustardy cheese is served on top of a slice of toast. Just add Worcester sauce and a dash of red pepper.

The address, 38½ Cornhill, isn't the only thing out of the ordinary about this 18th-century chophouse hidden down a narrow passageway. Thomas Simpson opened his Fish Ordinary Restaurant in Billingsgate market in 1723. He established a tradition, sadly now defunct, of "guessing the cheese". A whole cheese was wheeled in; whoever guessed the correct weight was treated to champagne and cigars. Simpson moved to this site in 1757. The original wooden booths, with brass rails to hang your bowler hat, can be wobbly when the portly punters have had too many pints. You have to share with strangers, which encourages plenty of boozy banter.

"What's an Edwardian pork chop?"

"It's very old – like the waitresses."

"Have you worked here long?"

"Not really – only 33 years", quips Maureen, still with a twinkle in her eye at 72.

Simpson's was the first establishment in London to employ female waitresses. Maureen, Iris and Nadia, a matronly trio in twinsets and pearls, cluck over their "boys" (most of whom are over 60) like mother hens. Blonde bombshell Trisha fends off advances in the upstairs dining room. Jean has been holding court in the basement bar for over 30 years. Yet female patrons were only admitted to the restaurant in 1916. The City traders still seem ruffled whenever I slide into a booth.

Once upon a time, two shillings would buy "the original fish dinner at 1 o'clock" – soup, four fish courses, two meat courses, bread, cheese and salad. Prices have gone up, but it's still remarkably reasonable. I guess the owners make all their money on booze: customers put away 50 boxes of wine a week, and it's only open for lunch, Monday to Friday. Friday lunchtime is liveliest, but do book ahead. Or you could write off the day even earlier with a "Full English" breakfast and a killer Bloody Mary.

WILTON'S MUSIC HALL  **19**

1 Graces Alley, Wapping, E1 8JB
- 020 7702 2789
- www.wiltons.org.uk
- Open Mahogany Bar Mon–Fri 5–11pm. Guided tours 3pm and 6pm every Monday. Check the website for performance times.
- Transport Tower Hill or Aldgate East tube
- Moderate

Sleeping beauty

Years ago, I went to Wilton's Music Hall for a wedding party. Decadent and dilapidated, layers of paint peeling by candlelight, the building almost stole the show from the bride and groom. Wilton's has a marriage licence now, so you can get hitched on the stage where knickerless girls once danced the can-can and performers ate live rats. This might not sound romantic, but Wilton's is dead sexy.

The oldest surviving Grand Music Hall in the world, this "shrine of gentle music" opened in 1858. John Wilton converted five terraced houses in an alley near Wapping docks into a hidden auditorium for cabaret acts. The

grand staircase was lined with hookers – "a better quality than the whores of Haymarket", according to one Victorian visitor. Punters had to buy a refreshment voucher from the box office; the minimum order was two pints of stout and a pie.

These days, patrons tuck into rum cocktails and takeaway noodles in the Mahogany Bar. Long since stripped of its mahogany fittings, the bar is a replica built for Guy Ritchie's Sherlock Holmes remake, which was shot here. Even so, the room oozes faded glamour. There are free acoustic gigs in the bar every Monday night. The main hall hosts a mixed bag of magic shows, film screenings, ping-pong tournaments and cabaret acts.

The music hall's heyday didn't last long. With industrialisation, the area soon became more slum than sauce. Wilton's giant chandelier with 27,000 pieces of crystal was sold off to cover running costs. The place closed in 1880. After trying to shut it down for years, the local Methodist mission moved in, staying until 1956. They served 2,000 meals a day during the 1889 dockers' strike, which spawned Britain's first trade union. Wilton's served as a refuge for anti-fascist protestors during the 1936 Battle of Cable Street, and a bomb shelter during the war. It would have been torn down to make way for council flats, if John Betjeman hadn't launched a campaign for the building to be listed.

Wilton's reopened in 2000, but decades of neglect have left it semi-derelict. £4 million is required for ongoing repairs. Run by a charitable trust that receives no public funding, the building's future is under threat. Go now and support this intriguing monument to East London's chequered history.

George Leybourne became an overnight sensation after his song "Champagne Charlie" was first performed at Wilton's. Moët & Chandon bought him a townhouse in Mayfair and paid him to drive through Hyde Park daily, drinking champagne in a carriage drawn by six white horses. He died of liver failure aged 42.

WAPPING FOOD

Wapping Hydraulic Power Station, Wapping Wall, E1W 3SG
• 020 7680 2080
• www.thewappingproject.com
• Open Mon–Fri noon–11pm, Sat 10am–11pm, Sun 10am–4pm
• Transport Wapping Overground or Shadwell DLR
• Expensive

> *A culinary powerhouse*

I f you can get beyond the arcane and impossible-to-navigate website, this intriguing restaurant and art space is well worth a visit. The Wapping Project is much less pretentious and more accessible than its online alter ego.

It opened in October 2000, the same year as Tate Modern – another power station converted into an artistic powerhouse. Built in 1890, Wapping Hydraulic Power Station harnessed Thames water to provide power to the surrounding docks and across London. During the heyday of hydraulic power, more than 33 million gallons of water a week were pumped beneath the streets of London, raising and lowering everything from Tower Bridge to the West End's revolving stages. When Wapping closed in 1977, it was the last power station of its kind in the world.

The restaurant is in the former Engine and Turbine Houses, raw industrial spaces with a patina of rust and decay, punctuated by red chairs and neon strip lights. Candles drip onto the tangle of pipes and engines. The crowd is a mixed bag of Japanese fashion students, a few suits, and plenty of arty intelligentsia.

Artistic director Jules Wright initially planned a one-off performance in the derelict space, but she fell in love with the building and raised £4 million to restore it. Site-specific performances and installations are staged in the Boiler and Filter Houses. Richard Wilson has crushed and rebuilt an aircraft on site, Anya Gallaccio installed a 34 tonne ice block, and Jane Prophet flooded the building with 70 tonnes of water. On our visit, Yohji Yamamoto had flooded the Boiler Room. A boatman rowed us across the inky water to watch a billowing wedding dress make waves.

These daring artistic experiments are funded by some very fine food. The chef is ex St John, so you can expect pan-fried offal, potted pork, and crispy pigskin on the menu. We skipped the meat-heavy mains and shared some simple but perfectly judged starters – broad beans, mozzarella and pea shoots, cured sea trout with cucumber and dill, and fried new potatoes with aioli. Only the offhand service left us cold.

The power station burns bright among the shadowy backstreets of Wapping Wall, but the area feels a bit Jack the Ripper after dark. Instead go for weekend brunch – buttermilk pancakes with raspberries and mascarpone, scrambled eggs with girolles and truffle oil on toast – followed by a stroll along the Thames Path. Or flop into the Prospect of Whitby, London's oldest surviving riverside pub, which opened in 1543.

JAMBOREE

Courtyard of Cable Street Studios, 566 Cable Street, Stepney, E1W 3HB
- 020 7790 1309
- http://jamboreevenue.co.uk
- Open Mon–Thurs 8–11pm, Fri & Sat 8pm–midnight, Sun 4–9pm
- Transport Limehouse DLR, bus 3D, 15, 115, 135
- Budget

Scout out new sounds

O n 4 October 1936, East Enders blocked the British Union of Fascists from marching through Stepney in the Battle of Cable Street. In the early 21st century, Cable Street became a battle of sound systems as techno raves, transgender parties and a fetish dungeon took up residence at Cable Street Studios, a 19th-century sweet factory converted into workspaces for artists and musicians. After a shooting in 2008, all the clubs' licences were revoked. The former techno club is now divided into a mosque and a toddler's playgroup, Gymboree – not to be confused with Jamboree, a live music venue tucked away in the courtyard.

There's no sign outside. Just follow the muffled strains of a fiddle into a shambolic wonderland that's part junk shop, part cabaret. "Most people want to keep it to themselves. We like it that way," says manager Rena Beck, a Swiss interior designer who had a studio on site. "I wanted to move into set design but it didn't work out, so I created my own stage." Beck's partner Alastair Clark, a sound engineer, wanted to give emerging bands a place to perform.

Originally the toffee-makers' canteen, the space was crumbling when they moved in. It took two weeks just to sand the floor. But they haven't tarted it up too much. The random ornaments are cast-offs donated by regulars or salvaged from skips – an accordion, a birdcage, an antique gramophone, a tableau of lampshades rescued from a pub that was being demolished.

Each night the line-up is different: it could be gypsy swing, Celtic folk or Costa Rican guitar. Sunday afternoons are devoted to Scrabble and vintage jazz. Monday nights are a raucous medley of bluegrass and folk bands. Most nights, a magician performs card tricks. In one corner, resident artist Armando Seijo paints live portraits of the bands and their fans, a rich mix of bearded folksters and dapper East Enders. It's always refreshingly lo-fi and unselfconscious. Dancing is spontaneous. Drinks are basic and cheap. Some events are free, for others there's a nominal entrance fee.

Like Wilton's Music Hall (see p. 144) at the opposite end of Cable Street, the building's survival is in jeopardy. The owner wants to demolish the studios to make way for more luxury flats for City workers. Long may the freewheeling artists and musicians remain in residence.

FAT BOY'S DINER

Trinity Buoy Wharf, 64 Orchard Place, Docklands, E14 0JW
- 020 7987 4334
- www.fatboysdiner.net
- Open Wed–Sun 10am–5pm (opening hours are erratic, so call ahead)
- Transport DLR to East India, then 10-min walk; bus 277
- Budget (cash only)

Mobile kitsch-in

Fat Boy's Diner is located in a "one-stoplight town" – a quiet sort of place, according to the dictionary of "dinerisms" on the menu. In a desolate corner of the Docklands, opposite the Dome, Trinity Buoy Wharf was named for the wooden buoys manufactured here from the early 19th century. It's still home to London's only lighthouse, built in 1864 to test maritime lighting equipment and to train lighthouse keepers. The old gas works and boiler rooms have been turned into workshops for carpenters and costumiers, and a community of artists and designers have taken up residence in Container City, colourful stacks of corrugated shipping containers. A photography and recording studio are housed in two lightboats moored nearby.

Parked between a primary school and a dance school, the red and chrome

mobile diner appears to have landed on the quayside from another time and place. It has: Fat Boy's was built in New Jersey in 1941. For 49 years, the diner was parked on the banks of the Susquehana River in Pennsylvania. After a stint at Spitalfields market, it relocated here in 2001. "There was nothing but tumbleweed then," says the Italian owner, Rosario Falcetta.

The bona fide interior, with its chrome bar and leatherette booths, is often used for film and fashion shoots. The cheesy menu also looks like the real deal: All American breakfasts, deli sandwiches, Southern Dawgs, and Fatburgers topped with Yellow Paint (mustard) or Brown Bad Breath (fried onions). The menu promises: "It's love at first bite", but sadly that wasn't the case.

"This burger tastes like it's from Iceland", my companion complained. Rosario had run out of buns, so his ABC (avocado, bacon, cheese) burger was served on sliced white bread – hardly the authentic experience we expected. My chocolate shake tasted of crushed ice and Nesquick. The menu advised us to ask our waitress about the daily specials, but she didn't speak a word of English. We didn't give her much gravy (a tip).

A rockabilly soundtrack would have perked us up, but the table-top jukeboxes don't work. So we wandered over to the lighthouse to listen to Longplayer, a mesmerising musical composition playing in real time, without repetition, for a thousand years. (Open every weekend 11am–5pm.) Next door is London's smallest museum, The Faraday Effect, a tiny hut celebrating the Victorian scientist Michael Faraday, who pioneered the electric generator here. Both are well worth the schlep to this riverside curiosity, even if the cardboard cheeseburgers are not.

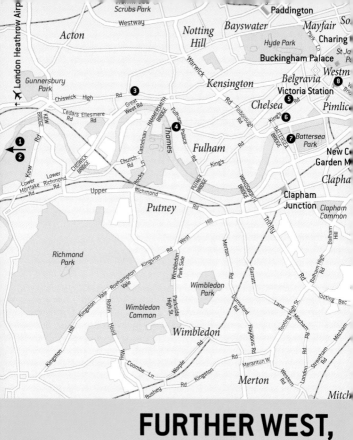

FURTHER WEST, SOUTH WEST, SOUTH & SOUTH EAST

GURDWARA SRI GURU SINGH SABHA

Havelock Road, Southall, UB2 4NP
- 020 8574 4311
- www.sgsss.org
- Open 4am–9pm daily
- Transport Southall rail
- Budget (free food, donations welcome)

> *Sikh and you shall find*

On a Sunday afternoon, there's a traffic jam on Southall's Havelock Road to rival Mumbai's Dalal Street, as worshippers stream into the largest Sikh temple in Europe. Sri Guru Singh Sabha opened in 2003 in Southall, London's "Little India". Asian immigrants first settled here in the 1950s to work at the local factories and nearby Heathrow airport. Predominantly Punjabis from north-west India, the population also includes Malaysian, East African and Afghan Sikhs.

London's first Sikh gurdwara (temple), was built in Shepherd's Bush in 1902. Today there are 15 gurdwaras in London, but this one is the most popular, attracting around 1,300 visitors daily and around 4,000 at weekends. With their sequined saris and giant turbans, the worshippers bring some pizzazz to the drab street of terraced houses. Colourful streamers flutter from the railings. The Sikh religion is founded on equality and rejects caste discrimination, so it's not surprising that non-Sikhs are welcomed at the temple. But be sure to follow the protocol: before entering the prayer hall, cover your head (scarves are provided), take off your shoes, and wash your hands.

After the service, a communal meal is offered in the *langar*, a spartan canteen where free food is provided for all, regardless of caste, creed, colour, sex or status. The kitchen is open every day from 5am until about 4pm, and dishes up around 1,000 meals on weekdays and up to 3,000 at weekends. Everything is donated, cooked, served and cleaned by *sewarders* (volunteers), backed up by a couple of professional cooks.

The food is pure vegetarian and the menu changes every day. Diners queue up with a compartmentalised metal tray, which is filled with dollops of dhal, vegetable curry, yoghurt sauce, sweet and sticky yellow rice, and flatbreads. Everyone eats side by side on strips of carpet on the floor. There's milky chai and sugary sweets for dessert. At weekends there's a greater variety of dishes, but never accept more than you can eat: leaving anything on your plate is considered disrespectful to the guru, upon whose generosity this bounty depends.

Donations – either in money or in kind – are welcome. Visitors can even help out in the kitchen, as long as they're freshly bathed and not inebriated. *Seva* – selfless acts of kindness or charity – is the essence of Sikhism and a visit to this temple is a gentle lesson in humility and generosity.

PALM PALACE

2

80 South Road, Southall, UB1 1RD
- 020 8574 9209
- www.palmpalace.me.uk
- Open Mon–Thurs noon–11pm, Fri, Sat, Sun noon–11.30pm
- Transport Southall rail
- Budget

Sri Lankan specialists

Southall is a vibrant little pocket of the Indian sub-continent on the Western fringes of London. Broadway, the main drag, bristles with fragrant spice shops, sari emporia, and street vendors manning sizzling vats of samosas, pakoras and jalebis. The dowdy Palm Palace is easily overlooked among the gaudy baubles and Punjabi curry houses that line South Road. Decorated with shiny tablecloths and forlorn fake roses, this Sri Lankan canteen promises a "Taste of Paradaise" on its website. If you have a fondness for Tamil food and a Teflon palate, then this is definitely heaven.

Palm Palace is one of the few places in London where you can sample freshly cooked *aapa* or hoppers, bowl-shaped pancakes made with rice flour and coconut milk. Like a lighter paratha with the texture of crumpets, hoppers are used to scoop and sop up smoky Ceylon curries, extra-hot sambols (Sri Lankan salsas), and *kothu* (a mish-mash of finely chopped meat, vegetables and *roti*, aka stir-fried leftovers). The hoppers were so irresistible that we ordered several varieties: glazed in extra coconut milk, topped with a poached egg, and drenched in honey. We didn't have room for string hoppers (a mat of red rice noodles) after gorging on mutton Ceylon, *paneer palak* (sizzling spinach and cheese in coconut cream), and *seeni sambol* (caramelised onion relish).

Smiling staff patiently explained the more obscure dishes. Although we requested all dishes to be served mild, everything was excessively spicy; but also astonishingly tasty and cheap. The menu is peppered with some rather creative spelling (the drinks menu features Brandi and Larger Chandy). Next time, I'll try the mysterious "chicken lollipop" and "chicken 65" (apparently made with a 65-day-old chicken, marinated in chilli, masala and ginger paste, and smothered in fried onions).

NEARBY

THE GLASSY JUNCTION

(97 South Road, Southall, UB1 1SQ; 020 8574 1626; www.glassyjunction.co.uk)

In Hinglish (Hindu-English), feeling "glassy" means you fancy a pint. Perhaps the expression derives from the Glassy Junction, a "World Famous Punjabi Pub" across the street, with Cobra and Kingfisher on tap and plasma screens showing Bollywood hits and Bhangra pop videos. It's the only pub in the UK to accept rupees as currency. Handy if you happen to have some spare rupees lying around; entertaining even if you don't.

LOWICZANKA

238–246 King Street, Hammersmith, W6 0RF
• 020 8741 3225
• www.lowiczankarestaurant.co.uk
• Open Mon–Fri 12.30–3pm, 6.30–11pm, Sat 12.30–3pm, 6.30pm–midnight, Sun 12.30–11pm. Reservations essential on weekends. Live music on Saturdays only.
• Transport Ravenscourt Park tube or 15-minute walk from Hammersmith tube; bus 27
• Moderate

> *Dumplings on the dance floor*

If you happen to love Boney M and schnitzels, Lowiczanka is the only place to be on a Saturday night. It is buried deep within the concrete bunker that is the Polish Social and Cultural Association (POSK), a hunk of Soviet-era brutalism that is the heart of London's Polish community. The POSK HQ contains a Joseph Conrad library, a jazz bar in the basement, and a member's club on the fourth floor. Anyone brave enough can visit the first-floor restaurant, Lowiczanka, but we were the only non-Poles on a Saturday night.

On first impression, we seemed to have wandered into a dinner dance on a dodgy cruise. There were gilt-edged mirrors, potted palms and dolled-up blondes. Once the Fantasy Band (a dour quartet of porky Poles) started up, it was more like we'd gatecrashed a wedding in Lodz. As the synthesised strains of Chris Rea belted out, there was a middle-aged surge towards the dance floor. By midnight, even the glamorous septuagenarians in skin-tight leopard-skin and fur stoles at the next table were getting down to a medley of 70s' disco, Polish pop and frenetic fiddling. The band segued breathlessly from *My Bonny Lies over the Ocean* to *Guantanamera*. The drummer even pulled off a plausible Louis Armstrong impersonation, with just a trace of a Polish accent. "This must be the Polish version of 'I will survive,'" said one of my companions, as the crowd went wild.

The menu valiantly keeps up the 1970s' theme. There are pancakes, sausages and schnitzels large enough to feed a family. Despite the disquieting images of fluorescent canapés on the restaurant's website, the food is surprisingly good. We slurped down cabbage borscht with sausage and clear beetroot broth - the perfect stomach-liner and liver-cleanser before we got stuck into the vodka. Shredded carrot, beetroot and cabbage accompanied hefty portions of potato rosti slathered with goulash and a lucky dip of *pierogi* stuffed with cream cheese and potato, sauerkraut and mushroom. The clear winner was roast goose in cherry sauce that fell off the fork and melted in the mouth. Dense poppy seed strudel came with a garnish of tinned peaches. How the other patrons managed to scoff such hearty food and then bounce around the dance floor was beyond me.

The only sour note wasn't the lashings of sour cream. It was the £60 unaccountably added to our bill. Our apologetic waitress blamed "the calculator", but I think the manager assumed we'd had too many vodka shots to notice.

MES AMIS

1 Rainville Road, Hammersmith, W6 9HA
• 020 7385 5155
• Open Mon–Sat 7–11.30pm
• Transport Hammersmith tube then 15-minute walk; bus 295, 211, 190, 220
• Moderate (cash only)

*A feast
for all senses*

Unless you happen to live locally or get lost looking for The River Café down the road, you won't stumble upon this little Lebanese local. The brilliantly bizarre interior looks more Mexican than Middle Eastern: stained-glass lanterns dangle from hand-painted ceilings suspended with parasols. Musical instruments, masks, paintings and plants jostle for wall space. Collections of cruet sets, teapots and stuffed toys are crammed onto every surface. Patterned carpets clash with chairs upholstered in loud florals. The fireplace is painted in primary colours. Tables are laid with spotted napkins, brocade tablecloths and fake bouquets. Even the toilet paper is printed with butterflies. To get to the psychedelic loos, you have to squeeze through a TV lounge lined with DVDs and old Elvis LPs.

This inspired interior is the handiwork of James Ilyas, a Syrian who arrived in Britain aged 11. The corner site was a boarded-up ruin when he moved in 20 years ago. Night after night, Ilyas presides over proceedings from his tiny open kitchen in the centre of the room. Dressed to kill in a glittery sweater, leather cap and bushy moustache, he looks like an ageing Village People impersonator. Ilyas works calmly, picking fresh ingredients from bowls on the kitchen counter. A pair of stuffed bunnies stands guard atop two towering jars of pickles.

The short bill of fare offers just three starters and seven main courses. "The menu reads like the corner kebab shop. You'd never expect food of this quality," said my companion, as we dunked and chomped our way through a spread of mezze. Smoky *baba ganoush*, delicately spiced meat samosas, zingy tabouleh and juicy kofte all disappeared quickly. Meaty mains are huge. Chicken shish kebab is drizzled in tahini sauce and served on a fragrant mound of chickpea, courgette and mushroom couscous. A minced lamb patty in yoghurt and tomato sauce garnished with blood orange and lime looks as good as it tastes. There's no dessert menu but a selection of bite-sized baklava appears on the house.

Our waitress Regina, a poised, gracious blonde, has worked here since the restaurant opened. With only a handful of tables, she knows most of her guests by name. "We've become friends with so many of our customers over the years," says Ilyas, who often makes special dishes for regulars. It's no accident that he called his deliciously eccentric establishment Mes Amis.

BARTS

5

Chelsea Cloisters, Sloane Avenue, Chelsea, SW3 3DW
• 020 7581 3355;
• www.barts-london.com
• Open Mon–Thurs 6pm–12.30am, Fri, Sat 6pm–1.30am, Sun 6–11pm
• Transport South Kensington or Sloane Square tube
• Moderate

Serviced apartments with hidden benefits

The dark heart of Chelsea is not the sort of place you'd expect to find a clandestine drinking den. Nor indeed is Chelsea Cloisters, a hulking block of serviced apartments rising above the expense account restaurants of Sloane Avenue. Only the building's 1930's architecture gives some clue to the speakeasy that lies within.

Stroll as nonchalantly as you can past the corporate, carpeted reception. On your left is a small black door with an inconspicuous sign. This leads to a booth disconcertingly lined with Mickey Mouse wallpaper and a neon sign for Tattoos & Piercing. Press the buzzer and eventually a flap in the door opens; it's like a gangster movie, only instead of a gun-toting meathead it's a hunky toff who lets you in.

Inspired by L'Esquina in New York – a tequila bar hidden below a taqueria – the venue used to be "a bar with a rather seedy reputation for nocturnal activities", according to manager Tom Foulser. The sultry space is decorated with junk shop curios: cuckoo clocks, vintage signs, and stuffed animal heads. The only concession to the Chelsea location is a trunk filled with wigs, hats and feather boas, catering to the Sloane Rangers' obsession with fancy dress. (Prince Harry would have a field day – and probably has.)

Behind the bar, a fuzzy TV plays old Charlie Chaplin movies. Boys in braces

and girls in glad rags dispense shots of absinthe with rum-infused fruit from the Thirst Aid box, or killer concoctions served in top hats and teapots, in line with the Prohibition theme. Signature cocktails have saucy names like Absinthe Minded and Tallulah's Tipple. The Charleston Crumble – rhubarb and pomegranate vodka martini – is especially addictive. As the menu warns: "Two or three of these and you'll be tapping and flapping all night."

The speakeasy soundtrack progresses from 30s' swing through to 80s' cheese. The crowd is international, but there's a real community spirit. Regulars are given their own key cards and priority booking at weekends, when the small space gets crammed. Even so, many people who live round the corner have yet to discover it.

Illicit pleasures include British comfort food – cheese on toast, sausage rolls, macaroni cheese – and Lucky Strike cigarettes. The cosy backyard is one of the sexiest places for smokers in London. But don't take the "Clothing optional beyond this point" sign seriously. It's cold out there. And if you look up at the winking windows, you'll be reminded that you're in an apartment block.

PHAT PHUC

151 Sydney Street, Chelsea, SW3 6NT
- 020 7351 3843
- www.phatphucnoodlebar.com
- Open Mon–Sat 11am–5pm
- Transport South Kensington or Sloane Square tube , then 10-15-minute walk
- Budget

Secret of a Spice Girl

I thought Uncle Wrinkle was the most bizarrely named restaurant in London. But that was before I discovered Phat Phuc. This Vietnamese noodle bar is much more appealing than it sounds. Situated beside Chelsea Farmer's Market, the clientele inevitably has a high quotient of Sloane Rangers and bankers' wives. But don't let that put you off either.

Long before London's recent obsession with street food exploded, this outdoor canteen was serving up steaming bowls of noodles to fragrant blondes. Hidden in a courtyard below street level, the ornate food cart strung with paper lanterns was brought all the way from China. But the short Vietnamese menu focuses on *pho* – the cleansing, soothing broth of vegetables and vermicelli flavoured with chicken, beef, or tofu that's served in countless food carts across Vietnam.

Traditionally a breakfast staple, *pho* is a very effective hangover cure (much better than a full English, and with none of the after-effects). Here, it can also provide sustenance on a freezing afternoon of shopping on King's Road. On a summer's evening, sitting at the trestle tables with a bottle of beer, you could almost be on a tropical holiday (although the umbrellas are more likely to protect diners from rain than sun in London's climate). When the bill comes to under a tenner, the name makes even more sense: Phat Phuc means 'Happy Buddha' in English.

Half the fun of eating here is sitting at the counter and watching the chef toss the ingredients of your soup into a giant pot, as you inhale the aroma of coriander, a whiff of lime, a splash of soy sauce. You can turn up the heat by dipping into the pretty little bowls of lethal chilli sauce. Besides the *pho*, equally delicious dishes are *bánh cuòn* (summer rolls with prawns or tofu), *bánh xeo* (steamed pancakes with crispy duck and hoisin sauce), and prawn laksa with coconut milk and lemongrass. Portions are so huge that I've never managed to squeeze in a slice of banana cake.

There are photos of the beaming owners with Kevin Bacon and Orlando Bloom beside the till. Apparently, ex Spice Girl Geri Halliwell has also been spotted here. But I doubt that any of these passing celebrities have qualified for a VIPP (Very Important Phat Phuc) Card, which gives loyal customers a 10% discount. If all those giant vats of noodles start taking their toll on your waistline, you can even buy a Phat Phuc T-shirt.

THE DOODLE BAR

33 Parkgate Road, Battersea, SW11 4NP
• 07866 629 908;
• www.thedoodlebar.com
• Open Mon–Tues 11am–7pm, Wed–Thurs 11am–11pm, Fri–Sat 11am–midnight, closed Sun
• Transport Bus 19, 170, 49, 319, 345 or 15–20 min walk from Clapham Junction station or South Kensington tube
• Moderate

Work in progress

Battersea isn't all second-class Sloanes and upmarket gastro-pubs. Behind Foster & Partners' glossy offices on the banks of the Thames, a creative community has quietly taken over the warehouses between Battersea Bridge and Albert Bridge. But you'd never know it was there. To find the studios where fashion designer Vivienne Westwood and architect Will Alsop are based, you have to go down a dark alley and through a car park, guided by a neon sign cryptically proclaiming Testbed1.

This former Victorian dairy and tile emporium was going to be knocked down to make way for more "luxury riverside living", but luckily the 2008 financial crisis foiled that plan. Alsop, an inveterate *bon viveur*, convinced the landlord it would be a good idea to turn a vacant carpenter's workshop on the ground floor into a bar for local staff. Alsop painted the whole space white and created The Doodle Bar – a blank canvas where patrons could scribble and sketch over every surface, including the waiters. This pop-up space has now graduated into a grown-up bar, but doodling is still encouraged. There are jars of coloured chalk for anyone who wants to make their mark on the columns, radiators, bar and a blackboard wall. The chalkboards are wiped clean every few days, with the best doodles preserved for posterity on the website. With so many designers, animators and architects in residence, and the Royal College of Art's sculpture department nearby, the competition is stiff.

The improvised aesthetic extends to the sandblasted walls, industrial lights, and furniture made from recycled Balinese boats. On the hidden terrace overlooking Ransome's Dock, there's a ping-pong table and a blacked-out old banger. Occasional events include life-drawing classes, "sketch mobs", and Wednesday evening talks on the likes of taxidermy, edible architecture and underground London. Bigger and crazier happenings are staged at the adjacent Testbed1, a vast, raw "space with no agenda", punctuated by distressed metal girders and strips of coloured neon.

Eventually, Alsop plans to build a kitchen; for now, you can bring gourmet lunch boxes from Street Kitchen next door. From noon to 2pm, two award-winning chefs produce phenomenal seasonal dishes at street-food prices, using ingredients sourced directly from British farms. (Street Kitchen's Airstream trailer also travels around the city dispensing lunch boxes – check http://streetkitchen.co.uk for details.)

THE VINCENT ROOMS

THE VINCENT ROOMS

The Brasserie
The Escoffier Room

Open Lunch time:
Monday to Friday
Table Reservations 12pm – 1pm

Open Evenings:
Wednesday and Thursday in the Brasserie only,
Table Reservations 6pm – 7pm

THE VINCENT ROOMS

Westminster Kingsway College, 76 Vincent Square, Pimlico SW1P 2PD
• 020 7802 8391
• www.thevincentrooms.com
• Open Brasserie: Mon–Fri noon–2pm and selected evenings 6–9pm;
Escoffier Room: Mon–Fri noon–2pm. Closed June–August
• Transport Victoria tube or rail
• Budget

School dinners

What's a pithivier? I have no idea and my waiter didn't seem to either. "It's a tart sort of thing with mushrooms and some sort of sauce."

Despite an obsession with obscure French culinary terms – Pont Neuf potatoes, *étuvée* of leek, sauce Périgourdine - the food at The Vincent Rooms is less fussy than it sounds. If the retro dining room, with floor-to-ceiling windows overlooking the leafy expanse of Vincent Square, has a school refectory feel that's not surprising: this is a catering school. Launched in 1910 to train chefs for the capital's luxury hotels, Westminster Kingsway College is the alma mater of many of London's chefs, including its most famous alumnus, Jamie Oliver.

The Vincent Rooms is actually two restaurants in one; both serve serious food at knockdown prices, cooked and served by catering and hospitality students. The flouncy Escoffier Room focuses on haute cuisine, with a seven-course tasting menu, featuring posh ingredients such as foie gras, snails and guinea fowl. Unlike the Escoffier Room, the more low-key Brasserie is occasionally open in the evening.

The menu changes every week and there are several choices for each course. The trainee chefs are clearly being put through their paces: most dishes come with elaborate sauces or wrapped in pastry. Disconcertingly, all the nervous, eager staff seem to be under-age. No wonder they can't open a bottle of wine – they're too young to drink the stuff. The mark-up on wines is very low, a good excuse to get sloshed if the food is hit and miss.

In fact, our supper was consistently good and occasionally brilliant. Poached egg tartlet with leek fricassee, black pudding and bacon crisp looked pretty and tasted pleasingly rich. Cream of white onion and fennel soup with orange mascarpone was an intriguing contrast of refreshing flavours. Pan-fried fillet of sustainable mackerel with potato tartare salad, baby carrots, Portuguese anchovy and chive *beurre blanc* was bright and light, though would have been better warm. My vegetarian friend was delighted with her red onion and chestnut polenta with cauliflower and stilton fritters, served with an endive, mango and Roquefort salad in a pomegranate dressing. Desserts were the only disappointment. Instead of bitter chocolate pudding we got what looked and tasted more like a meatball. At these prices, the occasional dud dish can easily be overlooked.

BRUNSWICK HOUSE CAFÉ ❾

30 Wandsworth Road, Vauxhall, SW8 2LG
• 020 7720 2926 • www.brunswickhousecafe.co.uk
• Open Mon 8am–5pm, Tues–Fri 8am–11pm, Sat 10am–11pm,
Sun 10am–5pm
• Transport Vauxhall tube and rail
• Moderate

A moveable feast

I f you find yourself desperate for sustenance on Vauxhall roundabout – a grim intersection between a highway, railway and bus terminal – a Tesco Express seems to be your only option. Yet lurking in the shadow of MI6's monstrous HQ, hipsters sip arcane cocktails in a courtyard stuffed with statuary, apparently oblivious to the rush of passing traffic.

Built in 1758, when Vauxhall was part of Surrey and Londoners flocked to its pleasure gardens to feast on ham and cheesecake, Brunswick House miraculously survived as the urban sprawl expanded around it. The crumbling Georgian mansion's fortunes were revived by Lassco, a salvage company specialising in "reclamation, ornament, curiosities", whose wares create a decadent backdrop for this laid-back restaurant.

The former ballroom is now the dining room, cluttered with colourful oddities: a cannon suspended from the ceiling, carved gold doors, bunting made from antique flags. Despite the preponderance of chandeliers, the lighting is pleasingly low. High-backed booths create a cosy set-up for foursomes. Most of the furniture is for sale, although Jackson Boxer, the young manager, has bought the basics. "If someone bought every chair in the building, we wouldn't be able to serve dinner."

Boxer grew up in the area. His father Charlie runs an Italian deli on nearby Bonnington Square. When Lassco suggested that Charlie open a staff canteen at Brunswick House, Jackson stepped in. With just enough cash for a coffee machine and a few cups, the business started small. Eventually, Jackson invested in an oven and began serving hot lunches. Evening trade took off as soon as he procured an alcohol licence, and now the restaurant is open five nights a week.

During the day, local workers pop in for gourmet sandwiches and soups. At weekends, brunch is served until 3pm. The daily changing dinner menu is inspired by what's available in New Covent Garden market nearby. "The menu is based around happy memories of all my favourite meals," says Jackson. This translates into delicious sharing plates influenced by different cuisines: purple sprouting broccoli dipped in romesco sauce, sizzling Jerusalem artichokes, wild mushrooms and melted lardo, crispy lamb's breast with plum ketchup. Portions are small, but so keenly priced that you'll happily order everything on the short menu (although you could skip the underwhelming puddings).

Jackson makes an occasional cameo in the kitchen, and "will do pot washing if required", but mostly you'll find him dashing about in bow tie and dinner jacket, running the show with panache.

BONNINGTON CAFÉ

11 Vauxhall Grove, Vauxhall, SW8 1TD
- www.bonningtoncafe.co.uk
- Cooks' telephone numbers on the website
- Open noon–2pm, 6.30–10.30pm daily
- Transport Vauxhall tube or rail
- Budget

> **An anarchic anachronism**

"**Y**ou don't come here for the food, you come to get progressively drunk and enjoy the atmosphere," my companion warned me as we sat down. This vegetarian cooperative won't dispel carnivores' preconceptions about vegetarian food as bland stodge that makes you fart. But the cosy, candlelit atmosphere really is special.

Like the other Victorian houses on Bonnington Square, condemned to demolition after being bombed during the Second World War, this one was taken over by squatters in the early 80s. Initially the café was a communal kitchen, because the squats didn't have gas, electricity or water. People paid whatever they could afford. Ingredients were leftovers from New Covent Garden market nearby.

Thirty years on, many of the properties (now worth over £1 million) are privately owned; the rest are run by low-rent housing associations. "It's a weird mix of old hippies and the super-posh, but they all come to the café," says Rachel Ortas, an illustrator who has been cooking here for 14 years. Still collectively run, the bohemian café hasn't changed with the times. There are purple walls, flowery plastic tablecloths and maps plastered on the ceiling. Prices are deliberately kept low, and are even cheaper at lunchtime.

With a different amateur cook every night, the cuisine and quality vary. There are about ten regular cooks and a waiting list of wannabe chefs from all over the world, so you might get a Malaysian, Italian, or even a medieval menu. My companion advised me to avoid the raw vegan supper. "After trying the 'zucchini linguini', I didn't come back for a year."

Tonight, there were just two choices per course. I chose "comfy chowder soup" (discomfortingly served cold) and gratin dauphinoise (a gloopy mass of overcooked potato drenched in tomato sauce). My companion struggled with a "Spanish platter" – a dry veggie burger served with rice and beans. I couldn't see where Spain came into the equation. A squidgy chocolate tart "didn't taste of chocolate".

Service can be chaotic: "If someone forgets it's their night to cook, then the café is shut," proclaims the café's manifesto. They don't bother with napkins. It's not just bring your own booze, it's bring your own salt. But our gripes dissolved when two French waitresses with ukuleles emerged from the kitchen to entertain us with a "*chanson classique*". Authentic and ad hoc, it's amazing that this idealistic relic has survived. You leave with a warm, fuzzy glow, even if you're farting all the way home.

RAGGED CANTEEN

Beaconsfield, Newport Street, Vauxhall, SE11 6AY
- 020 7758 6465
- www.beaconsfield.ltd.uk/cafe
- Transport Vauxhall tube/rail, Lambeth North, or Kennington tube
- Open Thurs, Fri 11am–4pm
- Budget

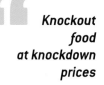

Knockout food at knockdown prices

Unless you're a fan of Portuguese restaurants and/or gay clubs, you might never have ventured into Vauxhall. Although only moments from the Thames and a short stroll from Parliament, this scruffy little patch of South London is marooned between so many ring roads that it's often overlooked. Fortunately, this has allowed Beaconsfield, an artist collective set up in 1995, to survive.

The tall, walled building sits incongruously among the mechanics who have set up shop in the railway arches lining Newport Street. It opened in 1851 as Lambeth Ragged School, a free school-cum-soup kitchen for impoverished children. Only the girls' wing has survived, as two-thirds of the school was knocked down to make way for the South Western Railway at the turn of the twentieth century. Later, the fire brigade used it as a rehearsal room for their brass band. During the Blitz, the windows facing Parliament were blacked out.

The exploding logo outside is a sign of what's in store: a gallery that blows up people's preconceptions. Ring the buzzer and it's a welcome surprise to find punters chowing down on vegetarian food in a yard that's hidden behind the high brick wall.

Inside the café, an informal space with flagstone floors and whitewashed walls, folksy music burbles above the satisfying thrum of spirited conversation. Daily specials – falafel burgers with sweet potato wedges, squash, ricotta and sage ravioli, spicy peanut soup – are chalked up on a blackboard. There's always a vegan and gluten-free option, as well as a selection of tempting toasties and cakes. Everything except the cakes is produced in the tiny open kitchen by chef Tim Laskey, whose eclectic recipes are "begged, borrowed and stolen from all over the place". "It's quite rough and ready," he cheerily admits. "We didn't even have an oven for the first year and a half." The herb garden on the roof supplies some ingredients; the rest are as locally sourced as possible.

Portions are huge and most dishes cost less than a fiver. "We're deliberately affordable," Tim explains. "But we don't actually make any money, which is a bit of a problem." The café was added in 2008 as a way of luring more people into the gallery. The clients are a mixed bag of local residents, artists, mums and workers. "Well, the more adventurous workers who are willing to brave the arts and cross the threshold of strangeness," smiles David Crawforth, who co-founded Beaconsfield. "The art is often challenging and political."

Certainly, you needed a strong stomach to watch chilling footage of the civilian victims of drone strikes in Waziristan in the gallery upstairs. Thankfully, I soon recovered my appetite with a delicious slice of Victoria sponge.

SIRENA'S

Southbank House, Black Prince Road, Vauxhall, SE1 7SJ
- 020 7587 0683
- www.sirenas.co.uk
- Open Mon–Fri 8am–5pm
- Transport Vauxhall tube
- Budget

> *Old china and a cheesy Italian*

In 1815, John Doulton invested his life savings of £100 in a small riverside pottery in Lambeth, an area with a long tradition in ceramics. Royal Doulton, which specialised in decorative stoneware and salt-glazed sewer pipes, became one of the largest potteries in England. The Lambeth factory closed in 1956 due to clean-air regulations, but part of the original premises survives, its striking façade embellished with ornate tiles.

The building has been rebranded Southbank House, an office block for PR and lobbying firms. Outside, a model of a midget chef alerts observant passers-by to the Italian restaurant hidden in the basement. Sirena's website promises "the atmosphere is friendly and unconventional", a description that turns out to be spot-on. Follow the lively chatter and whiff of garlic down a staircase lined with posters of the Amalfi coast. Sirena's opened in 1991, but the decor is more 1971. There are pink carnations and garlands of garlic. There's a takeaway sandwich counter for the office slaves who eat at their desks. You'd be crazy not to stay for the cheap pizza, tasty pasta and wisecracking waiters wielding phallic pepper grinders. If only every office had a staff canteen like this.

"*Buongiorno signora!*" bellows Carlo Raia, the ebullient Neapolitan manager. "I hope the food is good – sorry about the company." The menu is a catalogue of 1970s' classics: prawn cocktail, *melanzane parmigiana*, *pollo alla Milanese*. Pasta dishes cover all bases – amatriciana, arrabiata, alfredo – and some more unusual choices like "Rigatoni My Way" (tomato, peas, mushrooms and a dash of cream). There's more than a dash of cream in my carbonara, which comes drenched in béchamel. The situation is swiftly rectified with a heart-shaped Principessa pizza on the house. "Sweets from the trolley" are another artery-clogging extravaganza – tiramisu, lemon profiteroles, crème caramel.

"*Caffe per lei?*" asks the waiter, as he "spills" a fake cappuccino over my companion. A wooden birthday cake is whipped out for a bewildered regular's 85th birthday. "If everybody sing happy birthday I give 10% discount!" Carlo booms. There's surely no jollier way to kick off the weekend than lunch at Sirena's on a Friday afternoon.

NEARBY

TAMESIS DOCK
(Albert Embankment, Vauxhall, SE1 7TP; 020 7582 1066; www.tamesisdock.co.uk)
There's live jazz every Monday night at this Dutch barge moored between Lambeth and Vauxhall Bridge. The look is hippy-trippy, but the view from the deck is sensational.

GARDEN CAFÉ

Museum of Garden History, Lambeth Palace Road, SE1 7LB
- 020 7401 8865
- www.gardenmuseum.org.uk
- Open Mon–Fri 10.30am–5pm; Sat & Sun 10.30am–4pm; lunch served noon–3pm; closed first Monday of every month
- Transport Westminster, Waterloo or Lambeth North tube, then 15-minute walk. Bus 3, 344, 360, 507 or C10
- Budget (cash only)

A riverside revelation

"**A**nn Boleyn's mother is in the café," says one elderly matriarch to another matter-of-factly. The Garden Museum, housed in the medieval church of St Mary's at Lambeth, attracts ladies of a certain age who share an unhealthy obsession with gardens. The horticultural artefacts may appeal to a niche market, but the colourful salads and cakes on display in the museum café will be hard for anyone to resist.

On a busy roundabout by Lambeth Bridge, St Mary's was the site of over 26,000 burials including Boleyn's mother Elizabeth Howard, Captain Bligh of *The Bounty*, and the great 16th-century gardener John Tradescant. The church was deconsecrated in 1972 and destined for demolition to make way for a coach park. The altar, bells and pews had already been removed when Rosemary Nicholson came to the rescue. She set up the world's first museum of garden history in Tradescant's honour.

Wall-mounted tombstones surround the café, but leafy oilcloths and freshly picked posies on every table brush away any sense of impending gloom. The vegetarian menu changes daily according to what's in season. Salads, herbs and edible flowers are picked straight from the vegetable patch. Medlars and quinces come from the 12th-century orchards of Lambeth Palace next door. Everything else is sourced within 100 kilometres of London. The inspired food could convert the most militant carnivore: vegetable soup with basil and hazelnut pistou; fennel and cherry tomato gratin; courgette, pea and mint fritters; roasted sprout and beetroot salad. It's like Ottolenghi without the pretension and at half the price.

Sorrel Ferguson (what better name for a chef at a garden museum?) manages to look like a 1950s' pin-up despite cooking everything single-handed. Only the cakes are made by her lovely front-of-house team. Orange, almond and rosemary or courgette, ginger and lime cakes sound deceptively healthy, but are wonderfully decadent. Best of all are giant buttermilk scones (Sorrel's grandmother's recipe), served with clotted cream and stewed rhubarb.

An ancient door leads to a little knot garden planted with flowers that Tradescant grew four centuries ago. There's only space for about 20 in this secret sanctuary. If the matriarchs have got there first, take your lunch across the road and sit by the river. Plans for a purpose-built café in the garden are afoot, but for now Sorrel will continue to work miracles in her tiny kitchen.

MARIE'S CAFÉ

⑭

90 Lower Marsh, Waterloo, SE1
- 020 7928 1050
- Open Mon–Sat 7.30am–10.30pm
- Transport Waterloo, Southwark or Lambeth North tube
- Budget

> *Sweet and sour bacon and eggs*

Although it's full of market traders and cab drivers on a midweek morning, this isn't your average greasy spoon. The chilli sauce on the counter alongside the ketchup and brown sauce is the first clue. The blackboard menu may be all liver and onions, steak and kidney pie, eggs bacon chips and beans, but pinned on scraps of paper around the nicotine-coloured room are less traditional "daily specials" – sweet and sour prawns, fish ball soup, lychees and ice cream.

Marie's Café may look like the real deal, from the vintage signage to the original grease-stained counter, but its Italian namesake retired 25 years ago. A team of friendly Thais moved in. They didn't change much, apart from the addition of a few peeling posters from Thailand's tourist board circa 1980. After mastering the art of a good fry-up, the new owners gradually added a few

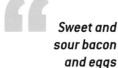

Thai specialities to the menu. Now Marie's becomes a fully-fledged Thai restaurant after 5.30pm.

The evening menu is long and occasionally hard to decipher. "Home Specials" include "crispy filler of cod", "homedal chili sauce", and "prawns in tamerian sauce". Starters tend to be oily, but fish cakes in chilli and peanut sauce are pleasingly squeaky. Salads laced with fresh chillies will bring tears to your eyes, but the curries are fairly mild. Green chicken curry and chicken penang both stand out, and the pad Thai is delicious. The sweet waitresses are always smiling (especially when they have no idea what you're saying) and you can bring your own booze.

NEARBY

SCOOTER CAFFE
(132 Lower Marsh, SE1 7AB; 020 7620 1421)

If the rough-and-ready atmosphere at Marie's doesn't cut it, order a takeaway and eat it at this idiosyncratic bar down the road. There's no sign outside: to find it, look for the vintage scooter in the window and the red neon sign proclaiming BAR among the second-hand shops and food stalls of Lower Marsh. Formerly a Vespa garage with a tiny espresso bar, this ramshackle joint has morphed into a cosy café-bar. The 1957 Faema coffee machine pumps out phenomenal hot chocolate and cappuccino. There are two resident cats, Stanley and Bob (Bob is a girl, who was born in the bar) and Peter the puppy occasionally pops in, too.

DA VINCI'S
(6 Baylis Road, SE1 7AA; 020 7928 8099)

This nondescript café becomes a dive bar after hours. Open until 4am seven days a week, it comes alive after the surrounding pubs and theatres close. You'll often spot stars from The Old Vic and The National Theatre getting down on the dance floor.

BUNKER BAR

The Old Vic Tunnels, Station Approach Road, Waterloo, SE1 8SW
- 020 7993 7420
- www.oldvictunnels.com
- Open Pre or post performances only – check website for details of upcoming events
- Transport Waterloo tube/rail, Lambeth North or Southwark tube
- Budget

Tunnel vision

The grimy, badly lit backstreets around Waterloo station aren't the sort of place you want to be wandering around after dark. Most nights, only junkies, tramps and muggers prowl the area. Occasionally, though, you might see gangs of fashionably unkempt youths traipsing down Station Approach Road. Follow them and the darkness suddenly gives way to a technicolour tunnel lined with graffiti.

In 2008, Banksy recruited the world's best graffiti artists to transform a disused railway arch on Leake Street into a work of art. Kevin Spacey and his right-hand man, Hamish Jenkinson, strolled over from the Old Vic theatre to watch the artists at work. Looking for a bathroom, Jenkinson stumbled on a labyrinth of abandoned subterranean railway tunnels. Although filled with junk and rubble, he was quick to spot their potential as an underground arts space.

The Old Vic Tunnels opened in February 2010 with the première of Banksy's movie, *Exit through the Gift Shop*. The Screening Room, with its art deco cinema seats, is a now platform for emerging songwriters, silent opera and improvised comedy, run mainly by volunteers. The other bare-brick

tunnels – still dank, decaying and decadent – make a spooky setting for all sorts of immersive, subversive productions, performances and installations. One night there's a live set by the New York Dolls; the next you'll find a pop-up restaurant manned by a European team of Michelin-starred chefs. Secret Cinema transformed the vaults into an Algerian souk. With a resident photographer, graffiti artist, designer, filmmaker and DJ, as you explore the vaults you never know what's around the corner.

Whatever the calibre of the performance, you won't be disappointed by the bar. The Bunker - a nod to its history as a hideout during the Blitz – is like stepping into a Tim Burton movie. The bar itself is a collage of broken doors, drawers and shutters. The furniture – wonky mirrors, second-hand sofas – is a jumble of car-boot sale cast-offs. There are dead things in glass cabinets and what looks like a door into the underworld behind the bar. Punky girls dance on rickety tables or throw shapes in shadowy alcoves. Drinks are basic but refreshingly cheap. Admission prices for events are also deliberately low. If any venue can dispel the idea that theatre is the preserve of wealthy, white pensioners, then this is it.

THE BOOT & FLOGGER

10–20 Redcross Way, Borough, SE1 1TA
• 020 7407 1184
• Open Mon–Wed noon–8pm, Thurs & Fri noon–10pm; closed Sat & Sun
• Transport Borough or London Bridge tube
• Moderate

> **Vintage wines and punchable nuns**

This is not an S&M club; it's a wine bar. The suggestive name refers to an old corking device: the bottle was steadied inside a leather "boot" while the cork was "flogged" into place using a wooden mallet.

With its wood-panelled walls and wing-backed leather armchairs, The Boot and Flogger has the snug ambience of a gentlemen's club. Antique prints, wig boxes, and dusty bottles of vintage port decorate the warren of rooms. The decor may look Dickensian, but in fact it dates to 1973. Housed in a converted smokehouse, the bar was founded by the Davy family, a dynasty of wine merchants and innkeepers since 1870. Many of the customers have been coming since it opened.

"This place is unpolluted by youth," my companion nodded approvingly. "Everyone has a walking stick." Most punters also bear bushy eyebrows and the telltale signs of a lifelong love of fine wines. Wisely, well-priced wines by the glass are all served in large (175 ml) measures. The giant barrels behind the bar are no longer in use, but house champagne is served in silver tankards, which

keep the fizz colder for longer. There's a tantalising list of special wines and a cracking selection of sherry, port and Madeira.

The old boys soak up the booze with hearty plates of seafood, game or gammon, served with verve by motherly waitresses. More port is consumed with a generous cheese plate or Bramdean pudding, a rich concoction of crushed biscuits, raisins, cream, custard and lashings of sherry.

Despite the smoking ban, cigars are available for sale. Smokers retire to the courtyard, where the stables date from the building's previous life as a fire station. In those days, fire engines were horse-drawn, as were taxis, as an old sign inside attests: "New post chaises and able horses at the shortest notice."

The Boot and Flogger keeps odd hours: closed at weekends, it usually shuts at 8pm, though opening hours have recently been extended until 10pm on Thursday and Friday. As you totter out into the Southwark night, pay your respects at the Cross Bones graveyard across the road. This unhallowed patch of wasteland contains the bodies of over 15,000 paupers and prostitutes, more commonly known as Winchester Geese, buttered buns, or punchable nuns. The graveyard gates are cloaked in colourful ribbons and totems; a vigil for the outcast is held at 7pm on the 23rd of each month.

40 MALTBY STREET

40 Maltby Street, Bermondsey, SE1 3PA
- 020 7237 9247
- www.40maltbystreet.com
- Open Thurs, Fri 5.30–10pm, Sat 10am–5pm; closed all of August
- Transport London Bridge tube/rail then 10-minute walk; bus 188, 47, 381, C10
- Moderate

Counter culture

On Saturday mornings, London's gourmands head to Maltby Street. Here, in the bowels of Bermondsey, a row of railway arches has been converted into warehouses for a number of artisanal food suppliers, who were keen to escape the tourist trap that Borough Market has become. The cool, damp brick vaults make ideal storing and maturing conditions for cheeses, charcuterie, ales, and wines. On Saturdays, the arches double up as shops stocked with pricy but top-notch provisions. Here, you can taste some of London's finest street food: toasted cheddar, leek and garlic sourdough sandwiches at Kappacasein, custard doughnuts from St John's bakery, pear and bergamot ice cream scooped out of the back of La Grotta's customised three-wheeler. Or you can pull up a stool at the counter of 40 Maltby Street and sample chemical-free wines paired with seasonal nibbles such as caramelised pumpkin with pine nuts and sage butter or kohlrabi and mint salad, while trains rumble overhead.

Raef Hodgson, the precociously young owner of this low-key enoteca, sources most of the ingredients from his neighbours. Then again, he's related to two of them: his father owns Neal's Yard, London's most famous cheese shop, and his mother runs Monmouth Coffee. Hodgson's partner, Harry Lester, founder of the Anchor and Hope gastro-pub in Waterloo, handles the wine import side of the business. The constantly evolving list showcases low or zero sulphate wines from small-scale producers in Italy, France and Slovenia. The mark-up is reasonable and the staff adept at recommending wines by the glass to pair with your dishes. The joy is that every time you come you can try something different.

The food, like everything else, is unpretentious but quietly sings. From the tiny open kitchen, chef David Cook produces sweet leeks melted in butter, crunchy herb-crumbed sprats with homemade mayonnaise, slow-roast pork with quince aioli. We watched with dismay as various dishes were crossed off the blackboard. By the time we got round to dessert, they were all gone. Surprisingly, only the cheese plate was flat – no biscuits, chutney or dried fruit to lift the rather stingy portion.

Saturday afternoons are always busy. It's much more of an adventure to go for supper on Thursday or Friday evening – the area is deserted and the wine bar glows like a beacon in the fog. But be warned: they don't take bookings, it's bar service only, and annoyingly there's no queuing system once you arrive – it's just a case of who has the sharpest elbows. So go early and be prepared to put up a fight.

THE LOBSTER POT

3 Kennington Lane, Kennington, SE11 4RG
• 020 7582 5556
• www.lobsterpotrestaurant.co.uk
• Open Tues–Sat noon–2pm, 7–10.30pm
• Transport Kennington or Elephant and Castle tube
• Expensive

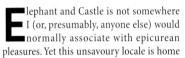

*Crustacean
sensation*

Elephant and Castle is not somewhere I (or, presumably, anyone else) would normally associate with epicurean pleasures. Yet this unsavoury locale is home to one of South London's most endearing seafood restaurants. A dining room designed to resemble the inside of a yacht might seem like a half-baked idea, but anything that transports you from these grim environs is to be welcomed.

From the cardboard fisherman and "welcome aboard" doormat outside, everything is nautically themed at The Lobster Pot. The dining room is as compact as a ship's cabin, with wood-panelled walls and fishing nets draped from the ceiling. There are portholes through which real fish swim back and forth, and a soundtrack of squawking seagulls punctuated by the occasional blast of a foghorn. You expect Captain Haddock to leap out of the woodwork.

The menu is fishy and extremely French. There's butter with everything – brown butter, lemon butter, garlic butter. Chef-proprietor Hervé Regent hails from Brittany, although his wife (and head waiter) Nathalie is from Mauritius, which accounts for the appearance of coconut and Cajun spices in some dishes.

Regent is almost comically Gallic, with slicked-back, soot-black hair and what looks like a stick-on moustache. When I ask whether there are any fishermen or chefs in the family, he shrugs. "Non, I hate my mother and she hates fish – so go figure."

Reeling them in since 1991, The Lobster Pot has a loyal clientele who come for the quirky ambience and heaving platters of *fruits de mer*. Watching half a dozen oysters, a tangle of langoustines, a vat of bouillabaisse, and half a lobster disappear down my date's gullet is a rather alarming spectacle for someone allergic to shellfish. But everything meets with his approval: "The langoustines taste like they've just crawled out of the sea." My fish soup is oppressively rich (apparently because it contains conger eel) and is served with sweaty cheese that's definitely not gruyère. But my entrée of char-grilled red mullet on buttered leeks with a slab of anchovy cream is an exceptional combination of punchy flavours.

Nathalie is an adroit hostess, but young staff in ill-fitting naval uniforms seem all at sea. Beside us, four dolled-up Asian girls struggle through the eight-course "surprise" menu. Nathalie harangues one of them for filling up on bread (who can blame her when the tasting menu features dodgy fillers like cheesy puff pastry and fruit salad.) Even if you order *à la carte*, you'll be stuffed after ploughing through the huge portions – but with an oversized bill to match.

UPSTAIRS BAR & RESTAURANT

89b Acre Lane (entrance on Branksome Road), Brixton, SW2 5TN
- 020 7733 8855
- www.upstairslondon.com
- Open Tues–Sat from 6.30pm; kitchen closes 9.30pm Tues & Wed, 10.30pm Thurs–Sat; bar licensed until 1am Tues & Wed, 2am Thurs–Sat
- Transport Brixton or Clapham North tube
- Expensive

> *Dinner chez Philippe*

With its inconspicuous entrance and intimate setting, Upstairs feels more like a supper club than a restaurant. Hidden in Brixton's backstreets, there's no sign outside, just a discreet buzzer on a residential street. As the door opens onto a narrow, carpeted staircase, unadorned apart from a couple of pot plants, the sense that you're entering someone's flat is heightened. A diffident young waiter waits on the first-floor landing to take your coat and offer you a drink in the small, rather soulless bar. We skipped aperitifs and headed up to the equally small second-floor dining room. Despite the soft lounge music and candlelight, the space is fairly spartan – cream banquettes, plain white crockery, bare walls. Large windows overlook Acre Lane's unglamorous shops – Leway nails, Handyman's Corner, Nairobi hair salon – with Big Ben and Centrepoint glittering hazily in the distance.

The French owners, Philippe Castaing and Stephanie Mercier, also run the ground floor café, Opus. With only nine tables, the prix-fixe menu (which changes every two weeks) is suitably succinct: three choices per course, with one meat, fish and vegetarian option for the starter and main course. The tasting menu includes samples of most dishes, paired with wines. If the location is unlikely, the quality of the food is even more so. The laconic menu is misleading: each dish is an elaborate composition of surprising delicacy, containing several unexpected ingredients. "Goat cheese mousse and hazelnut sable" turned out to be a creamy dollop of tangy cheese on a crumbly hazelnut biscuit scattered with bitter radicchio, endive and preserved grapes and served with apricot bread. Sometimes the surprise is less welcome: if you're not partial to black pudding, you'd be horrified to discover that "lamb rump with hotpot potatoes" is served on a bed of blood sausage. The tender lamb was more satisfying than a bony little fillet of mackerel with sautéed and puréed Jerusalem artichokes, topped with a lemon foam and raw wild rice that didn't taste of much. Quince cake with kaffir lime and cardamom ice cream covered with crunchy filo flakes was an intriguing blend of sour, salty and sweet.

The almost comically French maître d' described the composition of every dish in such a treacly accent that we had no idea what we were about to eat. But no matter: the subtle flavours spoke for themselves.

LISBOA GRILL

256a Brixton Hill, Brixton, SW2 1HF
- 020 8671 8311
- www.lisboagrill.net
- Open Mon–Thurs, Sun noon–10.30pm; Fri, Sat noon–midnight
- Transport Brixton tube, then bus 45, 109, 118, 250
- Moderate

*Funky
chicken*

Alas, the STOP! CHICKEN sign outside this clandestine Portuguese restaurant is no more. However, the heaps of whole grilled chickens splayed in the window of the smoke-filled takeaway might cause you to stop in your tracks. Not long ago, those in the know would go through the back door of the takeaway to a secret dining room. Despite the addition of a lurid cafeteria serving custard tarts and *pudim caramel*, through which you now access the restaurant, there's still nothing to alert passers-by to its existence.

Lisboa Grill was formerly known as The Gallery, presumably because of the garish murals of Portuguese landmarks and landscapes that cover the walls and ceiling. "It looks like somebody's child has painted the Sistine Chapel," my friend pointed out, rather unkindly. The rest of the room is a kaleidoscope of extreme tiling in beige, brown and green. Carefully folded napkins and dead carnations decorate every table. A mezzanine gallery overlooks the main dining area that sometimes doubles up as a dance floor – there's occasional live music, but mostly it's Portuguese pop or spontaneous outbursts of song. "We once waited so long for our main courses, we'd drunk so much wine we all launched into an impromptu rendition of *Edelweiss*," my companion confessed. Service may be slow, but it's unfailingly friendly. Most of the staff have been around since George and Maria Vidigueira set up shop in 1993; it's very much a family business and a popular outing for local Portuguese families.

The selection of Portuguese wines (including sparkling Vinho Verde, listed as "green wines") is impressive and very fairly priced. Everything on the menu seems to contain seafood, sausages, or salt cod. The special *cataplana* dishes, cooked in a giant copper pot, combine all three. Vegetarian options are pretty much limited to omelettes in various guises. But if you love chicken and chips, this place is paradise. Our waitress steered us away from the baby chicken – "a bit skinny; too many bones and veins" – and instead brought half a chicken in spicy *piri-piri* sauce buried beneath a heap of chips (sadly pre-cooked). If you're feeling daring, ask for *jedungo* sauce, which comes in a terracotta pot scrawled with the warning: "V. HOT". Succulent grilled prawns needed no condiments, but the cook was coy about the delicious marinade: "Only what God put inside." Gargantuan portions will please greedy people, but a starter and main course would be ample for two to share.

WHIRLED CINEMA

259–260 Hardess Street, Brixton, SE24 0HN
- 020 7737 6153
- www.whirledart.co.uk/cinema
- Doors open 7.30pm, screenings 8.30pm Thurs, Fri, Sat
- Transport Loughborough Junction rail; bus 35, 45, 345, P4
- Budget

*Up
the Junction*

Brixton has become cool again, since a flurry of top-notch food stalls set up shop in the covered market. Now you can feast on pad Thai, gourmet burgers or biodynamic salads before a screening at the wonderful Ritzy Cinema. It's all jerk chicken rather than satay skewers around Loughborough Junction, a scruffy patch on the rough outer edges of Brixton; but local residents do have their own secret cinema.

It's not easy to find. You have to navigate a tangle of tyre shops as you come out of Loughborough Junction station. Most of the railway arches are occupied by mechanics, but down a grungy alley, between a boxing gym and a Pentecostal church, a blue neon sign welcomes you to Whirled Cinema. Press the buzzer and a steep staircase leads straight into the 60-seat screening room. With its sandblasted brick walls, leather benches and cosy lighting, it has the intimacy of a home cinema. There's no box office, just a small bar where you can order pizza from Firezza, artisan ice cream and posh popcorn.

Manager Rob Lindsay is on first-name terms with all the regulars. A painter and courier, Lindsay got involved after hiring one of the artist's studios in the adjacent railway arches. Studio founders Mike Atterby and Lee Edmonds wanted to convert this derelict arch into an event space. Lindsay jumped in. "I started thinking about my dream job and decided it would be running a cinema," he says. "It was very Mickey Mouse at first. We had no money." It's still staffed by volunteers who study or work in film.

Access is for members only, but it's a steal: £45 a year (or £30 for six months) gets you and a friend free entrance to at least 45 films a year. You can also buy a weekly membership on the night for £8 – valid for one, but still cheaper than the average cinema ticket. Recent world and arthouse films are screened every Thursday, Friday and Saturday. Rob hopes to expand this to five screenings a week, as Whirled's word-of-mouth following grows (500 members and counting.) It's first come, first served, so go early to avoid a last-minute scramble for a seat or you may end up perched at the bar.

After the credits roll, the crowd dissects the film over mojitos and margaritas, their lively chatter interrupted by the occasional train rumbling overhead. Don't worry: they jack up the volume during screenings to drown out the sound effects.

PASHA KYRGYZ KAZAKH RESTAURANT

Pasha Hotel, 158 Camberwell Road, Camberwell, SE5 0EE
- 020 72772228
- www.hotelpasha.com
- Open Mon–Fri 6–11pm, Sat, Sun 1pm–midnight
- Transport Elephant & Castle tube then 15 minute walk, or bus 148, 12, 35, 45
- Budget

*Quite
a mouthful*

Walworth Road wilfully refuses to smarten up. Running into Camberwell Road, it's one long blur of Chinese takeaways, evangelical churches, nail parlours and fried chicken shops. I can't imagine why any traveller would choose to stay here, but the plucky Kyrgyz owners of Pasha Hotel beg to differ. "Follow the red carpet to reload, refresh and stay … to sharpen the saw and continue your journey", the brochure promises cryptically.

The entrance is a cross between a motel and a massage parlour. Black soap and sea sponges are dotted around the reception. There's nothing to indicate the presence of a restaurant, which is hidden at the end of a long corridor of rooms with "elegant furbishing", past a hamam, and a display of Kyrgyz costumes that wouldn't look amiss on a belly dancer. (Indeed, there's belly dancing on Fridays and live music on Saturdays from 8pm.)

A footbridge divides the colourful dining room, with a few aimless fish adrift in a pond. Seating is mainly on carpeted divans scattered with cushions. (Take my advice: don't wear a short skirt.) Central Asian pop is punctuated by the intermittent rattle of a train, which seems to run right through the restaurant.

Our endearingly cheerful waitress brought humus and fluffy flatbread while we dithered over the multi-ethnic menu. Inspired by the Silk Road, it's a medley of dishes from Kyrgyzstan, Kazakhstan and Turkmenistan, from *imam bayildi* to pickled herring. There's Georgian wine and Russian beer. Main courses focus on meat and stodge – kebabs, noodles, dumplings. Some dishes, such as lamb's tongue and chicken roulade with pickles, are only for the brave.

Our starters fell flat. *Olivie* (a salad of boiled beef, potato and egg mayonnaise) "tastes like school dinners", my companion sniffed. My stuffed vine leaves were mushy and bland. We perked up when the main courses arrived. Beef and onion *manti* (dumplings) with sour cream and kick-ass tomato sauce are made to order but were worth the wait. *Lagman* turned out to be "spag bol Krygyz style" – hand-made noodles with strips of spicy beef. *Plov*, spicy carrot pilaf with baked lamb, was much better than it sounded. *Chack chack*, billed as "the lightest of pastry desserts", was anything but light – "more like refried bits of *jalebi*". But with such gracious service, amazingly low prices and remarkable surroundings, I'll be back. I might even brave the belly dancer.

NO67

South London Gallery, 67 Peckham Road, Peckham, SE5 8UH
• 020 7252 7649
• www.number67.co.uk
• Open Tues 8am–6.30pm, Wed, Thurs, Fri 8am–11pm, Sat 10am–11pm, Sun 10am–6.30pm; closed Mon
• Transport Buses 12, 36, 436, 345, 171
• Moderate

Art de la table

Tracey Emin had her debut show at the South London Gallery, but don't let that put you off making the trip to Peckham to check out this innovative gallery and its brilliant café. Like the Whitechapel Gallery, the South London Gallery was set up by well-meaning Victorian philanthropists to bring a bit of high culture to the working classes. Apart from Camberwell College of Arts next door, the area is still a cultural wilderness.

Eating options are equally scarce, so it's not surprising that locals have embraced No67, a café in the gallery's new wing. A converted Victorian terrace, it would be easy to miss. "The architectural vision is to make it look like a house. Great for a gallery – not so great when you're trying to run a restaurant," says the young chef, Nick Hurdman. The dining room is small and intimate. Pendant lights cast a soft glow over bronze tables and elephant-coloured walls.

The laid-back vibe is perfectly suited to the food, which Hurdman describes modestly as "an extension of home cooking". He and his girlfriend Sam, who cooks during the day, have developed a cult following for their breakfasts and cakes. Surprisingly, few people have twigged that they also serve supper from Wednesday to Saturday. The gallery stays open until 9pm on Wednesdays and the last Friday of the month, so you can get a culture fix before dinner. Tables are set in a secret patio in summer.

The menu changes "on a whim", but it's always seasonal. Try to resist the delicious breads because portions are large and you'll probably be licking your plate, as my friend was when the smiling waitress slipped it away. Caramelised chicory and radicchio salad with feta, pomegranate and walnuts was a delicate balance of crisp and crunch, tangy and sweet. Parsnip soup with a swirl of truffle oil and a warm cheddar *gougère* was the perfect pick-me-up on a freezing Monday night. Wild bass with char-grilled cauliflower in caper breadcrumbs and a zingy romesco sauce tasted as good as a Spanish holiday. Curried beetroot with chickpea pancakes and raita was proof that vegetarian options are not token gestures. "Although beautifully executed and presented, it's not at all precious," was my friend's verdict as we polished off a flawless pecan pie. Only the intermittent whir of sirens reminded us that we were in Peckham. This is a proper neighbourhood restaurant – it's just a shame it's in this particular neighbourhood. Unless you happen to live here, of course.

THE BIG RED

24

30 Deptford Church Street, Deptford, SE8 4RZ
- 020 3490 8346
- www.thebigredpizza.com
- Open Tues–Fri 5–11pm, Sat noon–11pm, Sun noon–6pm
- Transport Deptford Bridge DLR or Deptford High Street rail. Bus 47
- Budget

Coach class "**D**eptford reminds me of Shoreditch ten years ago – rundown but on the cusp of becoming cool," says Albert Vega, the bashful manager of Big Red, a double-decker bus parked alongside Deptford Creek that doubles as a pizza parlour. If gentrification is happening, it's at a rambling pace: more dockside warehouses are being converted into artists' studios and galleries than luxury flats.

"An old Bristol bus had been languishing on this empty plot for years. I always hoped someone would do something with it – nothing happened, so

I decided to do it myself," says sculptor John Cierach, who owns the half-acre site. "Deptford seemed like a suitable place for something a little bit unusual, with so many artists from Camberwell and Goldsmiths colleges in the area."

So in summer 2011 Cierach created his "great big sculptural installation". Designed in homage to Lichtenstein, the double-decker bus crashes through a brightly coloured steel star. A cut-out doorway leads to a twinkly terrace wedged beneath the Docklands Light Railway track. With driverless trains hurtling overhead, it's like a scene from *Blade Runner*. Open all year, the creekside terrace is most appealing in summer; fresh mint is plucked straight from the flowerbeds for refreshing mojitos.

Cierach showcases new film, music, and art by local galleries and students in a blacked-out lorry parked out the back. Originally conceived as Lewisham Theatre truck – a movable cinema that screened movies in deprived estates – Cierach has converted the 40-foot vehicle into a creative hub for the community, with free admission. There are even bingo nights.

But the main attraction is the Big Red bus, fitted out like a Routemaster with original signage and the familiar chequered seats. Formica tables and red lights have been added to create cosy booths. The short menu focuses on straightforward pizzas at decent prices, simple salads and predictable desserts such as tiramisu. There are classic Margheritas for kids (the bus is a big hit for children's parties) and more adventurous toppings such as morcilla and chorizo or the Special Italiano (cured pig's cheek, buffalo mozzarella, Parma ham, capers and olives) to perk up parents. Wine, cocktails and ales from the nearby Meantime Brewery are all keenly priced. The bill comes in a bright red Oyster cardholder.

"If only the bus would start now and take us home to West London," sighed my date. That would indeed have been the perfect end to our foray into deepest Deptford.

FAN MUSEUM ORANGERY

12 Crooms Hill, Greenwich, SE10 8ER
- 020 8305 1441
- www.thefanmuseum.org.uk
- Open Afternoon tea: Tues & Sun 3–5pm. Museum: Tues–Sat 11am–5pm, Sun noon–5pm
- Transport Cutty Sark or Greenwich DLR, Greenwich rail
- Budget (but you have to pay the museum admission fee to have tea)

> *A fan-tastic tea room*

O ne of the smallest, strangest museums in London, The Fan Museum opened in 1991 but feels as though it's been here for centuries. Housed in two Georgian townhouses in Greenwich, the museum contains founder Hélène Alexander's exquisite collection of over 4,000 fans and related objects. (Even the soap in the bathroom is fan-shaped.) Most of the fans are stored in cedar-lined drawers to prevent damage and decay. The function of those on display varies wildly: fashion accessories, status symbols, ceremonial tools, political flags or advertising giveaways. At the apogee of their popularity at the turn of the 19th century, a whole "fan language" developed. A fan resting upon the lips meant "I don't trust you"; hiding the sunlight implied "You are ugly".

If the museum is a whimsical time warp, so is The Orangery tucked away in the garden. The whole room is decorated with a hand-painted mural of a pastoral scene, featuring a three-dimensional fan, *trompe l'œil* insects and flowerpots, as well as various Greenwich landmarks. Tables are daintily set beneath shimmering blue Murano chandeliers. Naturally, the napkins are decorated with fan prints. Peter Whittaker, the spry old house manager who lives on site, brings warm scones with clotted cream and plum jam made by Mrs Alexander. Full tea also includes simple sponge cakes or Bakewell tart made locally (but no sandwiches). In this enchanting glasshouse, you can't fail to slow down and feel that all's well with the world.

The Orangery is only open to the public four hours a week. Sadly, the delightful Japanese gardens, with their fan-shaped flowerbeds, aren't open at all thanks to the disobliging neighbours. This seems particularly churlish given that the museum only receives about 8,000 visitors a year, mostly grannies and fashion students. Even so, with only half a dozen tables, it's best to book ahead for tea, especially on Sundays.

NEARBY

OLIVER'S MUSIC BAR
(9 Nevada Street, Greenwich, SE10 9JL; 020 8853 5970; www.myspace.com/oliversmusicbar)
Intimate and shambolic, this is a late-night jazz bar in the old mould. Hidden down a gated alley, the black and red basement bar could be in Montmartre. Seasoned pros and precocious students from Trinity College of Music jam on the threadbare stage every night. The goateed Gallic owner, Olivier, serves "only liquid food, no fancy cocktails".

RIVOLI BALLROOM

346–350 Brockley Road, Crofton Park, SE4 2BY
• 020 8692 5130
• www.rivolilondon.com
• Open First Sat & first and third Sun of the month; check website for other one-off events
• Transport Crofton Park Station, Brockley rail/overground then 15-minute walk; bus 171, 172, 122
• Budget

Sex in the suburbs

It requires effort to reach the Rivoli Ballroom, but the schlep to deepest, dullest suburbia is worth it: this is surely one of London's sexiest venues. Despite its art deco frontage, you might walk right past the Rivoli, if it weren't for the vintage car parked outside. On either side of the entrance, two original signs read "Dancing" and "Tonight". People still come here to dance, but sadly it's no longer open every night.

The Rivoli opened as Crofton Park Picture Palace in 1913. Like many cinemas, it closed in the 1950s as television gripped the nation. After a makeover by local dance enthusiast Leonard Tomlin, it reopened as the Rivoli Ballroom in 1959. Tomlin's flamboyant interior – a riot of neoclassical, art deco and oriental motifs – is intact. A foyer with marquetry panelling leads

to the ballroom, a vaulted vision of scarlet and gold. The walls are lined with red velour and gilt encrusted with diamanté. Couples glide across the sprung maple dance floor, their sparkly frocks shimmering beneath crystal chandeliers, Chinese lanterns and disco balls.

Two bars flank the ballroom: one with red leather booths and an Arabesque tiled bar, the other with gold flock wallpaper and a mosaic ceiling. Even the etiquette is old fashioned: the barmaid calls you "Miss" and everyone waits in a single line to order drinks.

The first Sunday of the month is devoted to ballroom dancing, with owner Bill Mannix acting as DJ. Now in his 70s, Bill has run the Rivoli for over 30 years but none of the regulars have ever seen him dance. Everyone else does, though. Glamorous couples of all ages (the oldest stalwart, Ivy, is 92) foxtrot and quickstep across the room like Fred Astaire and Ginger Rogers. Many of the dancers have worked as extras on films shot at the Rivoli. (*My Week with Marilyn* and *One Day* recently shot scenes here.) It's occasionally used for concerts and music videos; Tina Turner and Florence and the Machine have both taken to the stage.

Regular events include the monthly Jive Party, with live bands playing vintage Americana. The evening starts with a jive dance class for beginners and ends with a rockabilly crowd sweating it out to lindy hop. At Jacky's Jukebox on the first Saturday of the month, men go into the ladies boudoir and come out dressed as women and the music segues from Louis Prima to *Saturday Night Fever*. Then there's The Magic Theatre, where guests must "dress to impress, astonish and entice" – just like the Rivoli Ballroom itself.

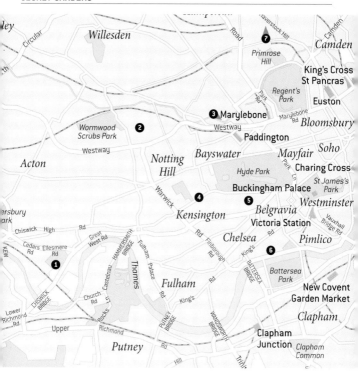

1 CHISWICK HOUSE CAFÉ

(Chiswick House & Gardens Trust, Burlington Lane, Chiswick, W4 2QN
• 020 8995 6356 • www.chiswickhousecafe.com)

Chiswick House, an 18th-century Palladian villa, provided a bucolic backdrop
for some of London's wildest parties. In 1844, the Duke of Devonshire
recruited four giraffes to entertain his 700 guests, including Tsar Nicholas I
of Russia. The minimalist café next door is a less extravagant affair, but it does
great breakfasts and is set in the glorious park where The Beatles shot the video
for *Paperback Writer*.

2 TUNG TONG . . . . See p. 75

3 THE CLIFTON KITCHEN

(Clifton Nurseries, 5a Clifton Villas, Little Venice, W9 2PH • 020 7432 1866
• www.clifton.co.uk)

You could easily lose a whole day at this romantic café in London's oldest
gardening centre. Tables are dotted among the shrubbery, surrounded by stone
putti and brilliant blooms, or set in a cosy greenhouse for chillier weather.

④ BABYLON

(The Roof Gardens, 99 Kensington High Street, Kensington, W8 5SA
• 020 7368 3993 • www.roofgardens.virgin.com)

100 feet above Kensington High Street is a one-and-a-half acre wonderland of Spanish, Tudor and English woodland gardens, with a fish-filled stream and four resident flamingos. Open since 1938, The Roof Gardens took two years to build at a cost of £25,000. They're now owned by Richard Branson, who added a members' club and restaurant, Babylon. The overpriced food is indifferent and the decor is Eurotrash, but it's magical in spring when the gardens are in bloom. The skyline stretches as far as Canary Wharf to the east, Crystal Palace to the south, and Richmond Park to the west.

⑤ OGNISKO

(55 Exhibition Road, South Kensington, SW7 2PN • 020 7589 4635
• www.ognisko.com)

This Polish émigrés' club has been around for over 70 years. Beyond the dining room is a secluded terrace overlooking Princes Gardens, where you can tuck into smoked salmon blinis, sweet cheese and orange pancakes, or work your way through the list of flavoured vodkas.

6 TANGERINE DREAM CAFÉ

(66 Royal Hospital Road, Chelsea, SW3 4HS • 020 7349 6464
• www.tangerinedream.uk.com)

The sweet and savoury treats are as heavenly as the setting in Chelsea Physic Garden, London's oldest botanical gardens. You'll have to cough up the hefty entrance fee to access the gardens (open April to October), but it's worth it.

7 BURGH HOUSE BUTTERY

(New End Square, Hampstead, NW3 1LT; 020 7794 2905
• www.burghhouse.org.uk)

Built in 1703, Burgh House is one of the oldest houses in Hampstead town. Now home to a small museum commemorating the local community, the basement café is a little known hideaway. On a sunny afternoon, taking tea and scones in the secret garden is like visiting an old friend's country house. Midweek, you'll only have the birds, the bees, and a few old fogeys for company. At weekends, you'll have to contend with the walkers striding off Hampstead Heath. The staff are friendly and the food is fantastic: feast on carrot, squash and ginger soup served piping hot in its own pot, with a warm buttered cheese and chive scone, macaroni cheese with herbed breadcrumbs, or lamb tagine with coriander couscous, while you fantasise about living in one of the surrounding townhouses.

8 CANDID CAFÉ

(3 Torrens Street, Angel, EC1V 1NQ • 020 7278 9368
• www.candidarts.com)

Candid Arts provides cheap studios and exhibition galleries for recent arts graduates in two crumbling Victorian warehouses on an Islington cul-de-sac. Upstairs is a bohemian café decorated with junk-shop finds, with a long communal table and a wall of windows looking onto a courtyard, a sweet little summer hideaway. Hippy tunes, lentil stew, gentle service.

9 GARDEN CAFÉ . . . . See p. 179

10 MUDCHUTE KITCHEN

(Mudchute City Farm, Mudchute Park, E14 3HP • 020 7515 5901
• www.mudchute.org)

London's largest city farm is in the least likely location – a muddy park overshadowed by the high-rise towers of Canary Wharf. The basic menu caters to mums with kids, who love the simple pasta and freshly made gelati. The Italian caterers, Frizzante, also run the kitchens at Hackney City Farm and Surrey Docks Farm.

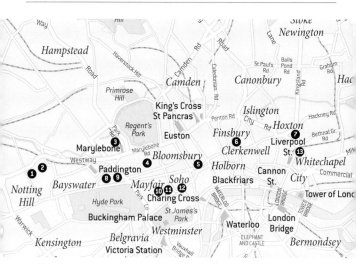

① BOOKS FOR COOKS . . . . See p. 83

② LUTYENS & RUBINSTEIN
(21 Kensington Park Road, Notting Hill, W11 2EU • 020 7229 1010
• www.lutyensrubinstein.co.uk)
This supremely stylish bookstore run by literary agents has an espresso machine in the basement so you can drink coffee in hand-made china cups decorated with the first lines of famous novels, while browsing the hand-picked book collection.

③ ALFIES ROOFTOP RESTAURANT . . . . See p. 99

④ PAUL ROTHE & SON . . . . See p. 33

⑤ CAMERA CAFÉ . . . . See p. 25

⑥ BRILL
(27 Exmouth Market, Clerkenwell, EC1R 4QL • 020 7833 9757)
Bagels, cappuccinos, and a brilliant selection of CDs make this the perfect little local record shop. Customers' top ten records posted on the walls are likely to inspire impromptu purchases.

⑦ PRUFROCK @ PRESENT
(140 Shoreditch High Street, Shoreditch, E1 6JE • 020 7033 0500
• www.prufrockcoffee.com)
Award-winning baristas knock up flawless flat whites in London's most exciting menswear shop. There are no seats, but coffee and clothing aficionados talk beans and threads at the counter.

8 ASSAL

(14 Connaught Street, Marble Arch, W2 2AF • 020 7706 2905)

Ladies who lunch toy with dainty cupcakes and cappuccinos at Cocomaya, but serious foodies prefer this Persian patisserie a few doors down. Pistachio and pine-nut cookies and sublime saffron ice cream are served with mint tea or cardamom coffee at a couple of tables on the pavement.

9 MARKUS COFFEE CO LTD

(13 Connaught Street, Marble Arch, W2 2AY • 020 7262 4630
• www.markuscoffee.com)

This delightful period piece has been supplying coffee to London's top restaurants since 1957. 34 varieties of beans (including their secret Regent and Negresco blend) are roasted on the premises daily, using the same Probata machine since the shop opened. The aroma is irresistible.

10 MILLER HARRIS TEA ROOM

(21 Bruton Street, Mayfair, W1J 6QD • 020 7629 7750
• www.millerharris.com/tearoom)

There are just four tables at perfumer Lyn Harris' Mayfair store, where you can linger over delicately scented infusions of violet, bergamot and rose petals. Everything is as elegantly packaged as her signature fragrances, from the floral wallpaper to the citrus and mauve teacups. The dark chocolate and sea-salt brownies are a revelation.

11 ROSE BAKERY

(17–18 Dover Street, Mayfair, W1S 4LT • 020 7518 0608
• www.doverstreetmarket.com)

The fashion world's favourite spot for secret trysts is on the top floor of Dover Street Market, Rei Kawakubo's avant-garde designer department store. The food is surprisingly good (and carb-rich) for a café that caters mainly for anorexics.

12 ARIGATO

(48–50 Brewer Street, Soho, W1F 9TG • 020 7287 1722)

This small but well-stocked Japanese supermarket is indispensable for sushi chefs. If you can't be bothered to make it yourself, the sushi counter offers fantastically fresh fish and great value bento boxes.

13 VERDE & CO

(40 Brushfield Street, Spitalfields, E1 6AG • 020 7247 1924
• www. verde-and-company-ltd.co.uk)

Jeanette Winterson's Dickensian corner shop is a work of art. Perch among the artisan olive oils and Marcolini chocolates and savour the small selection of exceptional sandwiches, salads and tarts.

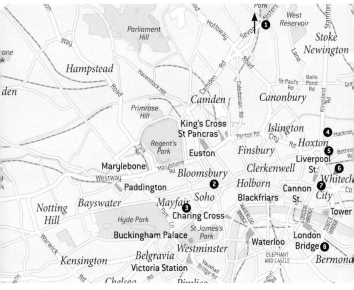

❶ MOSAICA

(Building C, The Chocolate Factory, Clarendon Road, Wood Green, N22 6XJ
• 020 8889 2400 • www.mosaicarestaurants.com)

It takes commitment to find this restaurant in the middle of an industrial estate in Wood Green. Once a chocolate factory that produced liquorice allsorts and sherbet fountains, the building is now a hub for creative enterprise. Sadly the food - sub-standard gastro-pub fare - doesn't live up to its surroundings.

❷ ARCHITECTURAL ASSOCIATION DINING ROOM. . . . . See p. 29

❸ SOTHEBY'S CAFÉ

(34–35 New Bond Street, Mayfair, W1A 2AA • 020 7293 5077
• www.sothebys.com/en/inside/services/sothebys-caf/overview.html)

The signature dish is the lobster club sandwich, which tells you all you need to know about this chichi meeting place for art collectors and Bond Street shoppers. Deliberately snobbish, it's just about affordable – unlike the rotating exhibitions of old masters and modern art on display, which inspire chef Laura Greenfield's excellent, ever-changing menu. The wine list, curated by Sotheby's resident expert Serena Sutcliffe, could do some serious damage to your credit card.

❹ THE PREMISES CAFÉ

(209 Hackney Road, Shoreditch, E2 8JL • 020 7684 2230
• www.premisesstudios.com/cafe)

Patti Smith, Jarvis Cocker, and Lily Allen have all recorded tracks at the music studios at the back of this brilliant little Turkish café. They're not the only fans of the fabulous mezze (and all-day breakfasts for Shoreditch ravers). Amazing value and genuinely welcoming, this place isn't just for groupies.

❺ ROCHELLE CANTEEN

(Rochelle School, Arnold Circus, Shoreditch, E2 7ES • 020 7729 5677
• www.arnoldandhenderson.com)

A school bike shed on Britain's first council estate might not sound glamorous;
but this is the office canteen for some of London's hippest fashion designers
and architects. There's no sign, only a discreet buzzer by the old Boys entrance.
Open for breakfast and lunch, the pared down menu focuses on finely tuned
British food - corned beef hash, Lancashire hotpot, bread-and-butter pudding.

❻ ARTS ADMIN BAR & CAFE

(Toynbee Studios, 28 Commercial Street, Whitechapel, E1 6LS
• 020 7247 6943 • www.artsadmin.co.uk/toynbee-studios/arts-bar-café)

Dancers, musicians and actors rehearsing upstairs refuel at this laid-back café
inside an arts charity. In summer, tables are set in the courtyard of Toynbee
Hall, the Arts and Crafts HQ of East End social reform since the 1870s.

❼ 40/30

(30 St Mary Axe, Spitalfields, EC3A 8EP • 020 7071 5008
• www.searcys.co.uk/4030thegherkin)

If you're lucky (or rich) enough to work at The Gherkin, you have access to the
members' bar and restaurant on the top three floors. The 360-degree views
from the glass dome, 180 metres above the City, are equally dramatic by day or
night. But you'll have to beg a member to get you in.

❽ MALTINGS CAFÉ

(Sarsons Brewery Works, 169 Tower Bridge Road, Bermondsey, SE1 3NA
• 020 7378 7961 • www.maltingscafe.co.uk)

Though the L-shaped dining room is a little clinical, the Italian food produced
by a friendly team in the open kitchen warms the heart. The brief menu,
which always includes phenomenal freshly made pasta, is chalked up on a
blackboard. Go early as food runs out fast.

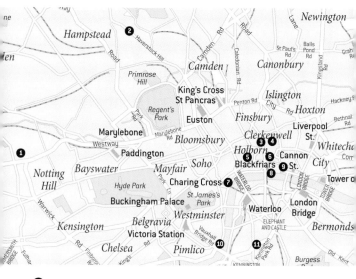

1　ARIADNE'S NEKTAR . . . . See p. 77

2　THE FREEMASONS ARMS
(Downshire Hill, Hampstead, NW3 1NT • www.freemasonsarms.co.uk
• 020 7433 6811)

The beer garden beside Hampstead Heath is always heaving in summer; but
the cellar of this rather corporate boozer is home to London's last surviving
skittles club. The object of this traditional pub game is to knock down nine pins
by lobbing (rather than rolling) a "cheese" (actually a thudding great ball of
lignum vitae). Matches are held on Tuesday and Saturday evenings. There has
been a skittles alley at The Freemasons Arms since the 19th century.

3　YE OLDE MITRE . . . . See p. 137

4　BREAKFAST AND BRUNCH BAR (COCK TAVERN) . . . . See p. 139

5　SEVEN STARS
(53 Carey Street, Temple, WC2A 2JB • 020 7242 8521)

Any pub with a landlady named Roxy Beaujolais deserves patronage. Inspired
by its location behind the Royal Courts of Justice, this snug watering hole is
decorated with legal curiosities. Even the resident cat, Tom Paine, is usually
dressed in a judge's ruff. The window displays ("cabinets of jurisprudence and
largesse") contain arrangements of bewigged skulls and stuffed mice. One of
several contenders for the oldest pub in London, the Seven Stars miraculously
survived the Great Fire, which broke out nearby.

6 THE VIADUCT TAVERN . . . . See p. 141

7 THE SHERLOCK HOLMES
(10–11 Northumberland Street, Westminster, WC2N 5DB • 020 7930
2644 • www.sherlockholmespub.com)

The mummified head of the Hound of the Baskervilles leers at the tourists
sipping pints of Sherlock Holmes ale in the bar. But the real surprise is upstairs,
where a faithful reproduction of Sherlock Holmes' study has been installed.
Created for the Festival of Britain, this shrine to the fictional detective has
been here since 1957. You can peer at Holmes' vials of borax, violin and
deerstalker through a glass wall in the restaurant. There's even a wax dummy
of the detective with a bullet wound in his forehead. Of course, the real Holmes
survived "to devote his life to examining those interesting little problems
which the complex life of London so plentifully presents".

8 COCKPIT TAVERN
(7 St Andrews Hill, Blackfriars, EC4V 5BY • 020 7248 7315)

"Any person with soiled clothing or dirty boots will not be served", says the
off-putting sign outside this tiny corner pub, tucked away below St Paul's
Cathedral. This is a bit rich, since the pub smells of wee; but it's worth poking
around if only for its history. Built on the site of the gatehouse William
Shakespeare bought in 1612, the pub used to be a cock-fighting arena. The
round saloon is the former cockfighting floor. Overhead is the gallery where
bloodthirsty crowds gathered to watch the "sport" until it was banned in 1849.
Traces of a Roman pizza parlour have also been unearthed on the site.

9 WILLIAMSON'S TAVERN

(1 Groveland Court, off Bow Lane, EC4M 9EH • 020 7248 5750)

The official residence of the Lord Mayor of London until Mansion House was built in 1753, Williamson's held the first excise licence in the City of London. Allegedly, an ancient marker denoting the dead centre of the City lies somewhere on the premises, but none of the staff know where it is. Browse the bound collection of *The Illustrated London News* and read all about the new "asylum for idiots" in Highgate or "the increase of pauperism" in 1849.

10 MORPETH ARMS

(58 Millbank, Pimlico, SW1P 4RW • 020 7834 6442)

Tate Britain was built on the site of Millbank prison, the first national penitentiary founded in 1816. Sadly, Jeremy Bentham's revolutionary "panopticon" design did not live up to his ideals of social reform. Henry James called Millbank "a worse act of violence than any it was erected to punish". Convicts bound for deportation to Australia were shuffled through a series of underground tunnels connecting the jail to the riverbank. A section of tunnel survives in the cellars of the Morpeth Arms, a pub built to serve the prison warders and allegedly haunted by the ghost of a former inmate.

11 PRINCE OF WALES

(Cleaver Square, off Kennington Park Road, Kennington, SE11 4EA
• 020 7735 9916 • www.princeofwaleskennington.co.uk)

Close to Oval cricket ground, this cosy pub is best known for the boules tournaments held in the pretty Georgian square outside.

12 THE BLIND BEGGAR

(337 Whitechapel Rd, Whitechapel, E1 1BU • 020 7247 6195
• www.theblindbeggar.com)

William Booth, founder of the Salvation Army, preached his first sermon outside the Beggar. But the pub is notorious for a more degenerate incident: in 1966, East End gangster Ronnie Kray walked into the bar and shot George Cornell dead. The record playing on the jukebox was *The Sun Ain't Gonna Shine Anymore* by the Walker Brothers.

ALPHABETICAL INDEX

Acknowledgements:
Thanks to Hannah Robinson, Gaby Agis, Jeremy Redhouse, Bill Nash, and especially Angelos Talentzakis for his huge appetite for life.

Photography credits:
All photographs by **Jorge Monedero** with the exception of the following who graciously provided their photographs: Ace Café, Atelier des Chefs, Barts, Bel Canto, Berry Bros & Rudd, The Big Red, The Boot & Flogger, Bunker Bar, Court Restaurant, Dinings, The Doodle Bar, Experimental Cocktail Club, Fat Boy's Diner, India Club, Knight's Bar, The Mayor of Scaredy Cat Town, No 67, October Gallery, RIBA, Rivoli Ballroom, Shayona, The Six Clerks, Upstairs at Rules, Upstairs Bar & Restaurant, Whirled Cinema, Wilton's Music Hall

Cover illustration: **Alice Charbin** · Maps: **Cyrille Suss** · Layout design: **Roland Deloi** · Layout: **Stéphanie Benoit** · Proofreading: **Caroline Lawrence** and **Kimberly Bess**

© **JONGLEZ** 2012
Registration of copyright: May 2012 – Edition: 01
ISBN: 978-2-36195-006-4
Printed in France by Gibert-Clarey
37 170 CHAMBRAY-LES-TOURS